MW00678698

GOD'S CONSTANT PRESENCE
True Stories of Everyday Miracles

Transformed *by* His Grace

GOD'S CONSTANT PRESENCE
True Stories of Everyday Miracles

Transformed *by* His Grace

EDITORS OF GUIDEPOSTS

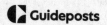

A Gift from Guideposts

Thank you for your purchase! We appreciate your support and want to express our gratitude with a special gift just for you.

Dive into *Spirit Lifters*, a complimentary booklet that will fortify your faith and offer solace during challenging moments. It contains 31 carefully selected verses from scripture that will soothe your soul and uplift your spirit.

Please use the
QR code or go to
guideposts.org/spiritlifters
to download.

Transformed by His Grace

Published by Guideposts
100 Reserve Road, Suite E200
Danbury, CT 06810
Guideposts.org

Cover design by Serena Fox Design Company
Interior design by Serena Fox Design Company
Cover photo by Cris Cantón/Getty Images
Typeset by Aptara, Inc.

ISBN 978-1-961126-38-1 (hardcover)
ISBN 978-1-961251-72-4 (softcover)
ISBN 978-1-961126-37-4 (epub)

Printed and bound in the United States of America
10 9 8 7 6 5 4 3 2

For it is by grace you have been saved, through faith—
and this is not from yourselves, it is the gift of God.

—*Ephesians 2:8 (NIV)*

TABLE *of* CONTENTS

———◦———

God Is Always at Work

Lawrence W. Wilson

TRANSFORMATION HAS BEEN elusive for me, something often sought but never found. I chased it over the long years of my early life, when time passed so slowly that it felt like a mirage in the desert. I can't tell you how many nights I bowed at an altar, praying the hymn "Fill Me Now," or how many days I confessed some sin, promising the Lord, "Never again!" or the number of times I'd knelt in prayer for the healing of my arthritic limbs, hoping to rise with a transformed body.

Yet nothing seemed to change. When I looked in the mirror each evening, I saw the same weak, broken human who had appeared that morning. After years of chasing this dream of a transformed life without success, I came to a sobering realization. Either I didn't understand what transformation meant, or it simply wasn't going to happen for me. Given that my concept of transformation was drawn from Scripture, the conclusions seemed obvious.

The images of transformation I saw in the Bible were bold, dramatic moments of stunning life change. Take Paul, for example. As Saul the Pharisee, he was a loathsome, self-righteous jerk. Saul was so blind to the truth that he actually went door-to-door hunting down Christians. That's what he was doing on the Damascus Road, riding forth like the Sheriff of Nottingham to round up believers and put them to death.

Then, *bam!* A blinding light. A voice from heaven. And Saul's life was forever changed. He was humbled, learning from the very people he'd been so eager to arrest. Where he'd once been impatient, even violent, toward people who disagreed with him, he was now eager to seek them out and welcome them into the faith. Sure, he argued with his critics, but he never wished them dead. He bore insults and even physical attacks without striking back. Everything about this man was changed, even his name. In one shining moment, Saul, the enemy of Christ, became Paul, the great apostle.

That's what transformation looked like, I'd always thought. It was John Wesley having his heart "strangely warmed" during a Bible study, then crisscrossing the British Isles, riding thousands of miles on horseback to preach the gospel. It was Chuck Colson, the Nixon hatchet man and Watergate defendant who met Jesus, admitted his crime, did the time, and became an advocate for prison reform. It was an alcoholic miraculously delivered from the desire to drink or the terminally ill person cured of cancer. I'd heard such stories and knew some of the people who'd experienced that dramatic intervention in their lives.

That was the experience I had looked for, prayed for, waited for, a divine moment that would so thoroughly change my heart, mind, and behavior that I'd never be the same. Yet after years of running up and down the Damascus Road, I never once felt "transformed." I had begun to despair of the thought that I ever would be.

Somewhere on the journey, I listened to a Bible teacher who pointed out something I'd not seen before. Not everyone's moment of transformation was instantaneous. Some of them took a bit more time, anywhere from a few minutes to a few years, sometimes even longer. And some of the stories were not as glamorous, shall we say, as the Apostle Paul's.

As one example, there was the man from the town of Bethsaida who asked Jesus for the same thing I'd begged God for countless times: healing (Mark 8:22–26). This fellow was blind. He asked Jesus to do something about it. We've seen this before. Jesus does something like touch the person, or sometimes just declares them well, and, voila! they can see, or walk, or stop hemorrhaging. Not this time.

First, Jesus took the man by the hand and led him out of town. Why? Jesus didn't say, and neither does Mark. But we get the idea it may be to keep the whole thing quiet. Then Jesus spit on the guy. Yes, spit on him, right in the eye. That's probably not what the fellow had in mind when he asked for help. Oh well. Jesus then laid His hands on the man and asked, "Do you see anything?"

The man said he did, but his vision wasn't quite 20/20. He saw people, but they looked like trees walking around. Was this a half miracle? A slow miracle? Transformation in little bits? Jesus laid hands on the man again. This time, when he opened his eyes he could see perfectly. So, yes, his sight was transformed. But it took a minute.

What happened next is a little troubling, in my opinion. Jesus told the man to keep this marvelous story to himself. So not only did he not go out to write a bestselling memoir and then hit the speaking circuit, but the man just went about his business. Stories like that have a way of getting around. But even so, this wasn't just a slow transformation. It was also a quiet one.

Reflecting on that idea, I found that I could see evidence of transformation in my life. It wasn't as dramatic as I'd wished, and certainly not as immediate. But God had placed people in my life to spit on me from time to time. For example, a cherished friend confronted me about my propensity to use sarcasm as humor, often at others' expense. "That actually hurts people's feelings," he told me. He wasn't angry. He was concerned about me and about other people. So he spat the truth straight into my eye.

And it worked. Little by little, I began to see the effect of my words on others, and to take greater care of their feelings. After a while the way I spoke began to change, a little at first, then all at once. It was a small change in my life—call it a half-miracle—but I was indeed changed.

Once I started looking, I could see more instances of ordinary grace in people's lives, and in mine. Zacchaeus is another. This height-challenged tax collector climbed a tree to get a better look at Jesus (Luke 19:1–10). Zaccheus was as small in mind as he was in stature. He had a zero-sum view of the universe in which every gain must come as a loss to someone else. He took that worldview to work every day, cheating people out of their hard-earned money by overcharging them on their taxes.

Jesus, entering the city, spotted the little guy in the big tree and decided to enlarge his thinking. Calling Zacchaeus by name, Jesus paid him a great honor by offering to share a meal with him. As a man who viewed the whole world with suspicion, we can imagine that Zacchaeus didn't have that experience often. And it broke his heart, in a good way. Zacchaeus was so moved by this act of kindness that he instantly passed it on, vowing to share his wealth with the poor and repay those he'd cheated.

Zacchaeus abandoned his scarcity thinking and began to see the world through the lens of God's abundance. To see other people as future friends, not enemies. Our wealth as a gift, not a right. And to remember that God always provides.

I remember the day I learned that lesson from Jesus Himself, disguised as a church lady. My wife and I had just had a second child and were preparing for a long journey to visit relatives. It promised to be a long, stressful drive in our small sedan. So this woman parked her brand-new minivan in our driveway, handed us the keys, and said, "Here, this should make your trip a little easier."

That moment changed my life. Like Zacchaeus, I'd had trouble wrapping my head around the concept of generosity. I considered tithing a legal requirement, like paying taxes. I meticulously calculated my tip at restaurants, never leaving a penny more than the minimum. Heaven help me, I even resented the Girl Scouts for hitting me up for a cookie purchase each spring.

All of that ended with the loan of that minivan. I'd been graced with a gift, and I was grateful. The only way to show it was to pass it on. Like the undersized tax collector who had dinner with Jesus, I now relish opportunities to show gratitude to God by blessing others. And when cookie season comes around, I buy as many as I can carry. A change of mind makes for a change of heart, which results in changed behavior. That's transformation.

Some of the transformation stories in the Bible are less playful than that of Zacchaeus. Some took decades to unfold. One of those is the story of Jacob, the man who wanted God's blessing perhaps a little too much. Jacob's frantic attempts to get hold of God's best remind me of all the ways my own zeal for God has been a thin disguise for self-interest. Yes, I've hungered for a transformed life. I've also wanted an easier, more comfortable life. It's easy to confuse the two.

Jacob, the brother of Esau, seems to have made the same mistake. He cheated his older brother out of the inheritance—material and spiritual—perhaps thinking he'd be set for life. Not so much. Esau, though not the brightest guy on earth, knew enough to realize he'd been had, and he became violently angry. Jacob was forced to flee.

In time, Jacob met a beautiful woman named Rachel and asked for her hand in marriage. Her father, Laban, was at least as shrewd as Jacob. For years the two wrangled over business matters, Jacob eventually gaining the upper hand. But once again, a hasty departure was required.

So Jacob headed back to his homeland, knowing that a showdown with Esau could cost him his life. Despite being a wealthy man with a large family, Jacob somehow understood that he'd still not achieved all that was possible for him. Uncertain of the future and knowing that he might well die the next morning, Jacob once again begged God for his blessing. Many of us have felt the heat of such a moment. Not knowing what lies ahead, realizing that the stakes are high for ourselves and our families, we make one last desperate plea that God will finally transform the mess we've made of our lives.

Jacob spent the entire night wrestling with God. And finally, after years of false starts and failures, Jacob received the blessing he had so deeply craved. But it came at a price.

Jacob's hip was painfully wrenched out of socket, causing him to walk with a limp for the rest of his life. Was he a changed man? Yes. Like Paul, even his name was changed, from Jacob to Israel. And his character was at last transformed. But the experience was not a coronation of Jacob's fondest hopes and dreams. It was a painful moment when pride and self-interest were finally stripped from his soul.

For some of us stubborn folk, transformation comes at the end of a long struggle. That can leave us marked in some ways by a painful divorce or a humiliating failure, or the loss of something we treasure. This kind of transformation is less a moment of triumph and more a moment of reckoning. But the result is just as thorough, and in some ways even more spectacular.

The butterfly is perhaps the most common metaphor for transformation, changed as it is from a crawling woolly worm into a delicate, colorful creature of flight. But that takes time and a kind of death. The old creature has to be stripped away to make room for a beautiful new one. By whatever the method, a little spit in the eye, a gift of grace, or painful cleansing, we can thank God for this sanctifying work in our lives.

One more example of transformation is Samson, the great strong man of the Bible. Samson is a story of wasted potential (Judges 13–16) that most of the men I know—and, I'm sure, many women—can easily relate to. This story is retold in any number of promising young athletes or entrepreneurs or preachers whose lack of discipline became their undoing.

Samson was gifted by God with unimaginable strength to be used as a protection of God's people. Instead, he used it to do party tricks and pick up girls. That ended in ruin as Samson was robbed of his strength, his sight, and his dignity, forced to labor like an ox for the very enemies he'd been commissioned to defeat. Stories like this make me want to cry, both for the tragic figures and their painful fall from grace and for my own mistakes, squandered opportunities, and talent too often wasted. Samson could have changed the world if he'd been able to master himself. That is perhaps the surest recipe for regret.

Thankfully, the story doesn't end there. Samson's gifting came at birth, but his transformation came at the moment of his death. The old champion of the Israelites, humbled by failure and haunted by regret, was finally in a position to be useful. With his pride and arrogance stripped away and his sight taken from him, he was at last able to see clearly. At the lowest point of his life, Samson summoned the courage to ask God for just one last chance. "Sovereign Lord, remember me. Please, God, strengthen me just once more," he prayed. His prayer was answered. And in one final act of courage, Samson accomplished more for God through his death than he had throughout his entire life.

As was true with Samson, some are gifted at birth but are transformed much, much later, at or near the moment of their death. Jesus said, "Very truly I tell you, unless a kernel of wheat falls to the ground and dies, it remains only a single seed. But if it dies, it produces many seeds" (John 12:24). We can also think of the fall trees, whose leaves display their brightest color only when dying. Sometimes, the greatest change, the most productive service, the most brilliant transformation occurs near the very end of life. That brings me hope.

It is never too late for my life to be transformed by the power of God. It's easy to think that some sins or flaws of character, ingrained habits or broken relationships can never be redeemed. Never believe it. There is no point in life when we are beyond the grace of God. Transformation is always, always possible.

Perhaps you, like me, tend to be more aware of the ways in which you lack transformation than of the ways you've been changed by God's grace. We often focus on the gap, not the gain. We measure ourselves by the ways we lack perfection rather than surveying the progress made. Seeking is good. Reflection is also important. Sometimes I like to think about the change in John the Apostle between his early days with

Jesus and his last writings, sixty or so years later. The same man who wanted to call down fire on villagers who would not receive Christ and who arrogantly asked to be seated next to Jesus in his Kingdom is the one who wrote, "Dear friends, let us love one another, for love comes from God" (1 John 4:7, NIV).

Think of Peter, the erratic, bombastic disciple who was ready to take up arms for Christ one minute and denied knowing Him moments later. He lived long enough to lead the church through a great persecution, and he remained faithful to the end. Tradition tells us that he not only submitted to crucifixion in Rome, but he also insisted on being placed on the cross upside down, not wanting his death to be compared to that of Christ.

Transformation happens. Sometimes in great bursts, sometimes little by little. Sometimes in our youth, sometimes along the way, and, for some, near the end of our lives. God is always at work, through the Holy Spirit, chipping away at our frailty, weakness, stubbornness, and sin, and replacing it with healing, humility, and holiness. Be alert to the people God places in your life and to the circumstances He puts you in. Some may be delightful, others painful. Each can be an instrument of transformation by the hand of God.

The work of healing is not my work, but by faith, healing is done ... It is not the works of righteousness which I have done, but according to His grace. I am a product of His grace.

—T. B. Joshua

CHAPTER 1

Healed by God's Grace

Quadriplegic No More

Adele M. Gill

As a chaplain and retired registered nurse, I have seen many miracles, great and small, but none like the one I witnessed when God healed my friend Gloria.

I had heard that Gloria had become a quadriplegic due to a spinal cord injury, and I went to visit her at the rehabilitation facility. As I entered her room, she was lying motionless in the hospital bed. Her arms and hands were on her chest, drawn up to her immobile body as if someone had placed them there, and her legs were slightly bent with a pillow underneath for support. Despite her seemingly desperate situation, she appeared upbeat and in good spirits as she reassured me she was OK.

"I've been praying for you ever since I heard about your fall," I told her. "Can you tell me what happened?"

"I fell down a flight of stairs at my parent's house," she replied. "The EMTs took me by ambulance to the hospital, where they told me that I had a spinal cord injury, and I'm a quadriplegic now. Since then, I haven't been able to do anything at all but lie in this bed. They sent me to this facility for physical therapy, but the doctors here told me they couldn't help me. So for the past six weeks, I've just been lying in my bed. They roll me every few hours, but I haven't done any PT at all!"

Gloria's voice cracked as she recounted what had transpired. Together we fought back the tears as she shared details of the tragedy she was living. I could hardly believe what I was hearing. Being a nurse, I knew well that the first six weeks after major trauma are critical to one's recovery. I was shocked and indignant that they had not tried to use that precious window of opportunity for physical therapy to help her.

After hearing her account of the accident, I asked if she would like me to pray with her. We had talked before about her faith in God, but I knew very little about her religious background and wasn't sure if she would be open to my prayers.

"Of course," she said. "I'd never turn down an opportunity for prayer."

"Good. If it's OK with you, I have a few questions before we pray."

"Sure."

I was curious to see if the tragedy she was enduring had affected her faith. "Do you still believe in God?" I asked.

She replied, "Yes."

> ### I believe; help my unbelief!
>
> —MARK 9:24 (RSV)

"Do you believe in Jesus, the Great Healer and Comforter?"

"I certainly do."

"How about miracles? Do you believe in miracles?"

"Yes, I believe in miracles. I hope I get one!" she replied enthusiastically.

Then I had just one more question: "Do you mind if I lay my hands on your legs as we pray and ask God to heal you?" Again, her response was a faith-filled, positive one. So I bent down, laid my hands on her upper legs, and began to pray aloud. I asked God to bring Gloria a swift and full physical healing, comfort, and peace.

After a few minutes of praying with her with my hands on her legs, she seemed uncomfortable and asked me to remove my hands, saying that they felt hot. That sometimes happens when I lay hands on people during fervent prayer. I removed my hands from her legs, and to my dismay, it looked as if she had a mild sunburn where my hands had been.

It took a moment for the obvious question to come to me: If she was quadriplegic, how could she possibly feel the heat from my hands? *Oh well,* I thought. *She must have been mistaken.* I ended the prayer, and we said our goodbyes. I gathered my walker and my ministry bag and headed for the door.

Before I reached the door, I turned around and looked back at Gloria to say something. I could hardly believe what I saw out of the corner of my eye. It was extraordinary, baffling, wonderful—and surely impossible. Her left foot had moved ever so slightly. But how could that be?

Excited, I turned my walker around and shuffled back over to her. The words came out of my mouth spontaneously, before I realized what I was saying: "Gloria, you're not a quadriplegic anymore!"

"Adele, what do you mean?" she responded, confused. She didn't know what I'd seen. "I know we just prayed and asked God for healing, but it is what it is. They told me I'm paralyzed permanently."

"No, Gloria, I'm an old neurology nurse and I know what I saw. God is giving you a healing miracle!" Then I asked her to move her foot again, and again her left foot moved ever so slightly. Now I understood why she had felt heat emanating from my hands onto her legs during prayer. This was a true healing miracle.

I was stunned, incredulous, and jubilant all at once. I was a firsthand witness to God's awe-inspiring presence, power, grace, and mercy. Though I had witnessed miracles many times before, this was the first time I had ever experienced one of this magnitude while it was still in progress.

Stunned, I went out to the desk to find a nurse or doctor, but after about fifteen minutes of searching for someone to tell, they were nowhere to be found. By that time, I was running late for another commitment and had to go. So I told Gloria what I witnessed and what was transpiring. I instructed her on exactly what to say to her health-care team—that she needed to be medically reevaluated as soon as possible, and why.

A few days later, I called Gloria to see if they had done the reevaluation yet. She said they had reassessed her and discovered that she was, indeed, no longer a quadriplegic. She was now a candidate for physical therapy rehabilitation. As her miracle and PT progressed over the coming weeks, I kept in close contact with her by phone.

> **For where two or three are gathered in my name, there am I in the midst of them.**
>
> **—MATTHEW 18:20 (RSV)**

Three or four weeks later, I went to see her. When I entered her room, to my pure joy, she was sitting up in a chair feeding herself. She was so proud, reveling in the miracle that was unfolding. Just a few weeks after that, she was discharged, and the social worker there at the facility arranged for her to move into an independent living apartment.

I called her to make arrangements to visit again, this time at her new apartment. "I have a surprise for you, Adele," she told me on the phone. "Don't come to my room. Stay in the lobby and I'll meet you there." I arrived on time and waited a while for her to come down from her room. When Gloria finally entered the lobby that day, she indeed had a big surprise for me. She had taken the elevator from her room down to the first floor, and then walked down the long corridor with her walker to meet me. Standing there, she was absolutely joyful

> **Then Jesus said to him, "Get up! Pick up your mat and walk." At once the man was cured; he picked up his mat and walked.**
>
> —JOHN 5:8–9 (NIV)

and radiant, reflecting both her huge accomplishment and God's unfailing help, His healing touch. We cried and laughed together right there in the lobby, celebrating her miracle.

Today Gloria continues to live alone in her own apartment. She still has some mobility issues and continues to use a walker. Fiercely independent, she uses a scooter to travel longer distances, even riding it down a side road to the grocery store two blocks away. Her new life is a far cry from the one she was living in the weeks just after her spinal cord injury.

By the grace of God, Gloria has had one of the most extraordinary miracles anyone could ever ask or hope for. I feel so blessed to have been an eyewitness to God's finest work in her. She and I will never forget the life-giving power of God's awe-inspiring, unmatched love, compassion, and mercy. It has only served to strengthen our Christian faith and bring hope to all who know her.

You Love Me Now?

Elsa Kok Colopy

I couldn't seem to shake it. I had picked up smoking cigarettes as a young teen, when I would ride my bike to the town pool and spend all day playing with friends. One of those "friends" had stolen cigarettes from his mother and introduced me to the habit. Back then it felt rebellious in a fun way. It seemed like such a grown-up thing to do. One afternoon I was smoking as I was riding my bike. An older boy came by and scoffed at me.

"You aren't even inhaling!"

I showed him! I hacked a few times, but ultimately I learned how to do it without coughing. Little did I know how quickly that would take me down the path to addiction. Soon, what I once enjoyed by choice became something I needed to get through the day.

Then my mom found out.

She was angry. Even worse, she was deeply disappointed in me. And she wanted to give me a strong enough consequence that I would truly let it go. After some thought, she told me that if I ever smoked again, I would not be able to work at the Christian camp I loved. She knew I was counting down the days to that camp—especially since there was a cute boy who I knew would also be working there. Yes, faith mattered, but at 16, the boy mattered even more.

I promised I would give it up. And I tried. Unfortunately, not even the cute boy was enough incentive. I was hooked, and so I simply became better at hiding it. Mints. Perfume. I tried everything to cover up the smell of my dirty little habit.

By the time spring rolled around, smoking had cemented itself into my world as a source of deep shame. I didn't want to lose going to camp, but I was genuinely addicted. One afternoon I was craving a cigarette badly. There was a small hole in the screen of my bedroom window, so I managed to light a cigarette and hold it there, blowing the smoke through the screen. My heart froze when the door cracked open behind me. I heard my mom gasp.

> **But God demonstrates his own love for us in this: While we were still sinners, Christ died for us.**
>
> —ROMANS 5:8 (NIV)

"Ze rookt!" she screamed to my dad in her native Dutch language. "She's smoking!"

The sob came up from the depths of me. I knew what it meant. My mom was furious. My dad was angry. I would not be going to camp that summer. I felt foolish and sad and ashamed and angry. The moment still stands out in my memory as one steeped in shame and sorrow.

Fast-forward ten years. I was now a single mom to a beautiful little girl. God had captured my heart, and authentic faith had sprung up out of the ashes of my poor choices. I truly wanted to live a life that honored God. I knew smoking was not a part of this new life, but I couldn't seem to give it up.

I was tremendously gifted at quitting—I quit nearly every other day. It just never seemed to stick.

I even promised my girl when, with her big green eyes fixed on mine, she pleaded with me to stop. Yes, I would quit. I should have known it never works to give up habits like that for anyone else. I made a good show of it, but I remember one evening sneaking outside after her bedtime. I sat on the back stoop and lit up a cigarette. Just in that moment, I heard a sound behind me. I turned to see her adorable little face smooshed up against the sliding glass window, disappointment in her eyes.

"Are you smoking, Mommy?"

Oh, mercy.

I felt awful. How many people was I going to disappoint before I set aside this stupid habit?

I quit again.

Months later, I went through a stressful season. Work. Family. Finances. Everything seemed to be piling up and I didn't feel like I was doing much of anything well. I felt the craving hit and didn't have the strength to set it aside. This time I went for a drive. I pulled out a cigarette, lit it, and took a deep, satisfying drag. Even as I did, I felt the shame pour over me. The embarrassment. The sadness.

It was late afternoon as I crested a hill close to my home. There, right in front of me, was the most spectacular sunset I'd ever seen. The colors were a vibrant mix of orange, red, and yellow. A few clouds added contrast to the bright beauty. It literally took my breath away. Fixing my eyes on that sunset, I felt God's love pouring out through the final rays of light. It filled me, flooded my heart, spilling out over and rinsing away my shame. I couldn't believe it.

GOD'S GIFT OF TASTE
— Buck Storm —

COMMERCIAL DIVING IS not always fun, especially when it seems there's more mud in the ocean than actual water.

Alone with the sound of just my bubbles, I was at a complete loss of sight. A black inkiness that no dive light could ever penetrate. And 20 feet below me a boat I had to somehow salvage.

Sometimes this world can feel as dark as a muddy dive. We grope in frustration, disoriented, feeling lost. But remember— He is not far from us (Acts 17:27–28). I surfaced that day to the sight of rough deckhands and a greasy dock. It was beautiful. How much more glorious it will be to one day step into the light of the Living God!

"You love me now?" I whispered.

I felt it in my heart and to my bones. *I love you ALWAYS.*

I lowered the window farther and tossed the cigarette into the street.

What shame had failed to accomplish, what consequences and disappointment did not do, love did in a vibrant sweep of orange, red, and yellow. This true, authentic, passionate, genuine love wasn't about my performance. It swept through, filled me up, and made me want to shine in return.

I left the cigarette smoldering on the road, and with it the shame that had plagued me for so long.

I was free.

A Medical Mystery and Angels Unaware

Bettie Boswell

It was winter. Everyone around us caught the flu or a cold. I had a bad cold. Some of my friends at work had the stomach flu. When my husband, David, suddenly became ill, we assumed he'd recover within a week. Instead, he continued to have bouts of intestinal problems that wouldn't go away. We tried the banana, rice, applesauce, and toast diet. We tried over-the-counter digestive cures. We tried chicken soup. When he suffered a fifty-pound weight loss within a month, we went to one hospital and then another. The staff ran test after test, but no answers or solutions for resolving the problem became apparent.

As David grew weaker, our prayers grew stronger. He began to discuss funeral arrangements as we prepared for the worst-case scenario. As Christians we hoped for God's peace in heaven, but yearned for a few more years together. In desperation, we begged our insurance company to allow a visit to a major clinic. We secured an appointment several months away. Miraculously, there was a cancellation and an earlier date opened up a week later. We would meet with the head specialist for intestinal issues.

David had always been the driver between us, but when the time came, he was so weak that I was the one who drove him across the state and through unfamiliar city streets. I pushed him into the clinic in a wheelchair because he couldn't walk. We were in awe of the amazing facility. However, after running more tests, the famed doctor had no answers. He suggested a visit with a specialist dietitian after his investigations proved nothing. Again, the earliest appointment was several weeks away.

> **So [Naaman] went down and dipped himself in the Jordan seven times, as the man of God had told him, and his flesh was restored and became clean like that of a young boy.**
>
> —2 KINGS 5:14 (NIV)

In the meantime God sent several friends to offer us other alternatives. A neighbor suggested herbal supplements, which helped some, but not much. Then two different friends, at two different times, suggested that maybe a gluten-free diet might help. One man's aunt had a similar problem and had given up using flour. Another woman's sister felt better when she avoided gluten entirely.

At first David refused to think about eating differently. Wasn't toast part of the usual diet for people suffering intestinal issues? These friendly advice givers were not doctors. What did they know when the professionals hadn't found a cure? In some ways David was like Job, sitting in his ashes and enduring well-meaning advice from those around him.

When more people suggested a gluten-free diet because of problems suffered by a friend or relative, a memory came to me of a coworker having a similar issue. The woman became very ill and lost a lot of weight. She chose to go gluten free and her health improved. I felt like God was answering our prayers through the multiple messages friends provided. I just needed to convince my husband to give the diet a try.

Like the leper Naaman, who didn't want to follow Elisha's command to dip in the water for cleansing, my David was reluctant to try this simple change at first. It sounded to him like a fad diet. And when we mentioned the idea of going gluten free to a doctor, the physician was dismissive, saying David would be eating bread that tasted like cardboard. David didn't like that idea at all. But finally he gave in to my pleas to at least give it a try.

Within a day, he could eat a meal that didn't immediately make him ill. In a week, his strength returned. He put down the cane he'd been using and started doing a few things around the house. By reading labels, we discovered his favorite candy, chocolate-covered peanut butter cups, was gluten-free. That information made him very happy, and it gave him hope that a permanent transition to the new diet wouldn't be so bad. God had answered David's prayers in an unexpected way.

> **When Job's three friends . . . heard about all the troubles that had come upon him, they set out from their homes and met together by agreement to go and sympathize with him and comfort him.**
>
> —JOB 2:11 (NIV)

By the time our dietitian appointment arrived, David had gained back quite a few pounds. When we arrived and told the doctor and his assistant that his improved appearance was due to a gluten-free diet, they were skeptical. After all, no blood work or other medical testing showed he had the gene for celiac disease, which would indicate that he was allergic to gluten. The assistant asked how I even knew how to prepare gluten-free food. When I mentioned looking up recipes on the internet, she reprimanded me for trying. Knowing our choice had worked, I chose to ignore her words.

> **Plans fail for lack of counsel, but with many advisers they succeed.**
>
> —PROVERBS 15:22 (NIV)

We left the office understanding God had provided an answer for us when the medical field had nothing to offer. I discovered that almond and coconut flour, along with a few additives, made decent bread. Those ingredients also worked for breading items like fried chicken or country-fried steak. Oat-based cereals became David's new staple for breakfast.

Several weeks later, we received a follow-up call. The dietary doctor had done some research and discovered that many people in the modern world were developing gluten allergies. Some medications caused the allergy, while other cases indicated reactions to genetically modified grains or chemicals used in processing wheat, barley, or rye. The dietary doctor's assistant offered me an apology during that call. She encouraged me to keep providing my husband with gluten-free food.

We still occasionally have issues with things like licking envelopes loaded with glutinous glue, or using a toothpaste with a wheat-based binder, but we are thankful to know what is causing the reaction. Now we read labels before buying new products. We've found breads that don't taste like cardboard. As more people discover they have the same allergy, food manufacturers are finding ways to make appealing gluten-free products. Laughter has replaced sadness when well-meaning friends confuse gluten with glucose and offer him sugar-free items filled with flour. In order to avoid cross contamination, when eating out at restaurants David has learned to ask for a cleaned grill and whether all products are fried in the same vat.

Thanks to our advice-giving neighbors and friends—our angels unaware—my husband has lived past those dark days where we worried about his well-being. We are grateful to the Lord, who saw our need and helped my husband transform his diet to live a long and healthy life.

God's Will, Not Mine

Pam L. Waddell

It had been a great year. I was enjoying my first grandchild. My career as an administrative assistant to the chief of police was going well. Being "Mama Pam" to all the officers in my city's police department had become my joy and calling. I was taking classes in computer programming, offering me even more job security. Life was good—until it wasn't.

My head was pounding when I woke up that February morning. I'd become used to that due to a stubborn sinus infection. I forced myself to get up and get going in spite of the pain, but then the room spun crazily. My legs and feet flopped as I tried to get to the bathroom, and I fell to the floor. Crawling to the phone, I tried to call my husband, but I couldn't remember his work number. I had to look up a number I had known for years!

Steve later told me my words were slurring as he helped me into the doctor's office. I couldn't make the pen move to sign in. *What is happening?* The nurses rushed me into an exam room and took my blood pressure—220/180. Dangerously high. My physician, Dr. McClanahan, burst into my room. After a quick exam and a few questions, he told Steve to take me immediately to Montclair Hospital. He had already made arrangements with a neurologist. As we left, Doc stopped me at the door and hugged me. Even through my brain fog and confusion, that told me something was seriously wrong.

Days later, after many tests, I still had no real answers. All the tests ruled out stroke, but the effects gave me stroke-like results. Finally, I returned home, unable to walk without support.

So began my yearlong recovery. My speech had returned, but my short-term memory was gone. Everything I had learned in the last six months of IT training had vanished! Every phone number I had dialed for years was gone! It was surreal.

A week later, during a follow-up, I asked Doc what had happened. He explained that my sinus infection had moved from my sinuses into my cerebellum. It was very rare—he had only seen it happen to two other patients during his career.

"How are they now?" I asked.

Dr. McClanahan looked at me and said, "Pam, they both died."

I was shocked. Now I knew why he had hugged me before sending me to the hospital! At that moment I knew God had a plan for me, or I would not have survived. I prayed, thanking Him for His mercy and grace.

It would be a few weeks before I could write my name and nine months before I returned to work part-time. During my recovery, I recalled the words of Psalm 56:3, although at the time I couldn't remember the verse number: "When I am afraid, I put my trust in you" (NIV). I recited it to myself over and over.

My friends gathered around me to support me. They prayed earnestly for me. They became my cheering section. When I got down, they picked me up. They drove me to physical therapy sessions. They encouraged me to set goals. The biggest goal was easy because my son was getting married in August. It was April at the time, and my goal was to walk down the church aisle on Wesley's wedding day on my husband's arm, not on my walker.

My daughter, Tracey, was always my encourager. When I received an invitation to a wedding shower, I hesitated. I had only gone to church and doctors' offices with my walker. Tracey told me to get dressed, because she was picking me up and we were going. On the day of the shower, she arrived with her fifteen-month-old son, Drew, in tow, loaded me and my walker into the car, and off we went. When we arrived, we slowly made our way up the sidewalk and into the house with Drew's little hand on my walker. I had to admit, it was nice to get out and socialize with friends I hadn't seen since my "non-stroke," as I now called it.

As the summer wore on, I made progress toward my goal. I could walk short distances without assistance, but my balance was way off. Any quick turn of my head sent me sprawling to the floor. My depth perception was also affected. Navigating steps or uneven pavement was especially difficult without help.

My best friend, Susie, decided to take me to the mall. She thought going up and down the escalator might help restore my depth perception. We walked along the upper level, allowing my vision to adjust to seeing different levels. After a while, the white-knuckle dizziness slowly diminished. Then we tackled the escalator. I'm sure people thought we were nuts as I hung on to the side for dear life, trying not to scream. Susie laughed as she held on to me so I wouldn't fall. We rode down, then up, then down again until I could go up and down without feeling like I was falling. Susie was a genius!

My vision changed almost weekly. My optometrist was kind and saw me biweekly to change my prescription to fit my vision changes. God supplied every need in all these things.

Two weeks before my son's wedding, I was cleared to drive! Feeling like a teenager who had just gotten her license, I drove the forty-five minutes to meet my future daughter-in-law, Micah, at the venue for their rehearsal dinner. On their wedding day, I proudly walked down the aisle on my husband's arm to take our seats. No walker needed!

I returned to work half-days in September, only two days a week. I was disappointed because I thought I could work more than that, but I didn't argue. The first day back was exhausting. The phones ringing and officers coming and going were more than my brain could handle. I couldn't remember the phone numbers I used to recite a hundred times daily. I had to look each one up. Strangely, I instantly remembered them once I looked them up. The human brain is amazing, as is our Creator God!

> **When I am afraid, I put my trust in you.**
>
> —PSALM 56:3 (NIV)

It would be almost a year before I was fully released to return to work full time. I settled into my new routine, happy to be working again. I had missed all the officers and my coworkers, even if the job was stressful. I accepted my physical limitations. I still had residual balance issues and was on blood pressure meds, but my vision had settled down. I loved being back at work. That year was lovely.

One Sunday night I began having chest pains. I ignored them, hoping they would stop. They got worse as my breathing became difficult. I woke Steve up and told him to call 911. The paramedics arrived quickly, and I was taken to the hospital for a possible heart attack. The tests found a defect in my aorta and an irregular heartbeat. A day later I was released and advised to follow up with Dr. McClanahan.

After a few weeks of rest at home, I returned to work. I was tired when I went home for lunch, so I lay down. My heart began to race, and the chest pains returned. Another ambulance ride and hospital stay led Dr. McClanahan to suggest it was time I retired from my job at the police department. He said it was a stressful environment my heart could no longer handle. I was devastated.

All the rehab and physical therapy and goals I had set to return to my job and now this. All my friends and colleagues. I loved my job! Who would I be if I wasn't Mama Pam? What did God want from me? Then I heard Him. *I know the plans I have for you…plans to prosper you and not to harm you, plans to give you hope and a future* (Jeremiah 29:11, NIV).

> # I can do all this through him who gives me strength.
>
> **—PHILIPPIANS 4:13 (NIV)**

I had learned to trust God fully in the two years between my non-stroke and my unwilling retirement. But this was different; this was my future. Did God want me to sit and do nothing? I couldn't! It was selfish, but I was accustomed to having my own spending money. Now, I would need to depend on Steve for everything. It was a humbling thought. After many tears and prayers, I gave God my worries and my future.

After I retired, I went through several different part-time jobs, but each one came with additional health issues. God has used each one to show me that His plan is best, and that I need to depend on Him and Him alone. He has never let me down. I've learned to trust Him fully in His will, not mine. Today I write, teach Bible classes, and counsel those going through the pain of grief. God is still proving He is trustworthy.

Craig's Miracle

Tina Wanamaker

One morning some months back, I picked up my phone and saw that my friend Cathy had texted me, wondering if I could visit the boyfriend of one of her employees, who was in the hospital.

I called Cathy, and she told me this man, Craig, hadn't been feeling well, and his girlfriend had taken him to the doctor. In the office, the doctor noted several concerning issues and instructed the girlfriend to take him to the hospital. Craig fell into a coma and became nonresponsive not long after they arrived. He was in atrial fibrillation, had some fluid around his heart, and also was systemically septic.

Craig was flown to Seattle, where they did all they could before sending him to a hospital in Richland, Washington, closer to his home. His family was called in, and the doctor recommended taking him off life support.

Cathy was almost four hours away from Richland. She had been in contact with Craig's girlfriend, and they both wanted him to be visited and ministered to. When Cathy asked the Lord who might go, I came to mind, which was what prompted her text to me. Although Cathy had done as much as she could for Craig, she wanted to make sure that the gospel was clearly presented to him before he died.

After praying about this and receiving an affirmative answer from the Lord, I texted Cathy back and told her I would go. Things fell into place wonderfully that afternoon. My children's homeschool lessons had wrapped up for the day, there was nothing for me to finish at home, and I was able to begin the hour-and-twenty-minute drive after lunch.

I arrived at the hospital, checked in as a visitor, and headed up to the floor, where I approached a nurse and found out where Craig was. When I walked into his room, I found a tall, burly man lying in bed, still comatose. I sat in a chair next to him, introduced myself, and asked if I could sit with him for a bit.

> **For God so loved the world that He gave His only begotten Son, that whoever believes in Him should not perish but have everlasting life.**
>
> —JOHN 3:16 (NKJV)

Of course, I got no response. Still, I knew that studies have shown that hearing is the last sense to go, and I always strive to demonstrate the reverence for life I find in our Lord. So I spoke to Craig in the same way I would have if he had been responsive. I held his hand and shared about God's great love for him, the sacrifice of Christ in giving His own life, and that Craig, too, could receive the gift of God, eternal life.

And then I began to pray for him. I can't recall all I prayed, but toward the end I said, while weeping quietly, "Lord, if it's Your will, would You please raise Craig up to glorify You." I sat with Craig for a while and reflected on who he was, what his life might have been like, and the brevity of our lives on this earth. He was only 61.

After a time, I felt released to leave with the knowledge that I had completed the task the Lord set before me. I believed God could use what I had shared, and that perhaps somehow Craig could place his trust in Him before he left this earth—even while in a coma. I headed home, expecting I'd get a call from Cathy in the next day or so, telling me Craig had died.

Cathy did call two days later. "Tina, I need to tell you something!" she exclaimed, brimming with excitement. "Craig's awake!"

Awake? I was so surprised I couldn't respond.

Again, she proclaimed, "Craig's awake!"

Craig had woken from his coma. Although still struggling with heart issues, he was talking and coherent. The medical staff couldn't explain it. Everyone seemed genuinely shocked. Not only was he awake, but his girlfriend said he was different. He was now thanking each staff member who helped care for him. This was not the Craig she knew.

> **The Lord is not slack concerning His promise, as some count slackness, but is longsuffering toward us, not willing that any should perish but that all should come to repentance.**
>
> **—2 PETER 3:9 (NKJV)**

As Cathy's words sank in, I shared with her about my visit and my prayer time with Craig, my sense that the Lord was ministering to him through me. We both cried at Craig's miraculous healing, at God's goodness, at the way He holds all of us in His hands. She asked me to consider visiting Craig again, and I told her I would pray about that.

Again, I felt confirmation to go. This time I asked the Lord why I was going, and He impressed upon my heart that a piece was missing for Craig. He now believed in God, but he still needed to place his faith in Christ.

> **From whom the whole body, joined and knit together by what every joint supplies, according to the effective working by which every part does its share, causes growth of the body for the edifying of itself in love.**
>
> —EPHESIANS 4:16 (NKJV)

The next day I drove back to Richland to see Craig. This time when I walked into his room, he was awake. I sat next to him, took his hand, and asked if he remembered my last visit. He didn't. When I asked if I could share what I had prayed over him, he agreed. I told him, "I prayed, 'Lord, if it's Your will, would You please raise Craig up to glorify You.'"

Tears welled in his eyes and then coursed down his weathered cheeks. "I know it was God who did this, who brought me back," he said.

I asked, "So you believe in God now?"

"Yes, I do," he said.

I gently asked if he was ready to place his faith in Jesus. He said he was, and he did so that day in that hospital room with me holding his hand.

GOD'S GIFT OF HEARING
— Heidi Gaul —

ACCORDING TO *NEUROSCIENCE NEWS*, the sense of hearing is the last sense to go during the dying process. Often, even in a coma, a person can hear and comprehend the sounds around them. I find this news heartening. The final words we share with loved ones are important. They offer us a chance to say goodbye.

While I sat with my mother as she lay dying, I told her how much I loved her. I felt comforted, secure in the knowledge that not only could she hear me, but also that the next voice she'd hear would be Jesus's.

Craig went on to share that he had been a mean kid who grew into a mean man. He didn't know why he was like that and didn't want to be like that, he said, but he was. He acknowledged that he hadn't lived his life for God but for himself and that he had been looking to his girlfriend to meet all his needs. It seemed like God had opened his eyes to all this while he was in the coma.

I sat with him for some time, holding his hand, praying off and on, and just being present. Finally, I felt it was time to go. I prayed over Craig, said goodbye, and quietly slipped out of the room and headed to my car for the drive home. Craig was released from the hospital a few days later.

A few months afterward, I got a call from Cathy that Craig had died. We knew he was now in heaven. She told me Craig had attended a funeral for one of his biker buddies about a month before and had told his old friends there, "I met Jesus when I was in that hospital."

As I consider these events and how they played out, I'm struck anew by God's perfect timing. God so loved Craig—a man who, by his own admission, had been mean and only interested in helping himself—that He performed a miracle by bringing him back from the brink of death to give him a second chance to place his faith in Christ. And He used the members of the body of believers to help that miracle work, prompting each individual to act at the right time and in the right order so that His plan would be fulfilled. The Lord had a plan—and that plan is still in motion as Craig's story is shared with others.

The Grace Warrior

Melissa Kirk

The line between keeping busy and overcommitting to too many activities had blurred, and I needed clarity. But I was too busy to notice.

My husband, Larry, and I were in the early empty-nest years, and I was seizing new opportunities. Alongside the joy of playing my newly gifted role as a grandparent, I decided it was also time to dedicate more effort to advancing my career as an insurance agent. Additionally, I took on responsibilities in our church by teaching a class and helping in the women's, children's, and music ministries. To fulfill my civic duties, I joined Kiwanis and served on the county's Chamber of Commerce board. Amidst it all, I always squeezed in time for my sorority.

My hectic schedule had morphed into a complex puzzle, and I eagerly embraced the challenge of piecing all my quests together in pursuit of the happiness that I and all my peers sought.

Then my mother was diagnosed with cancer, and I became her caregiver. Refusing to let go of any of my commitments, I expanded the borders of the puzzle to make more pieces fit, like trips for chemotherapy treatments and unexpected hospital stays. I would wake up long before sunrise and push relentlessly until I collapsed at the end of the day.

I sank into bed one night and dozed off before catching up on the evening news. I awoke a few hours later to discover my right arm was numb. It had been resting above my head on the pillow, so I used my other arm to move and massage it until a cold, tingling, awakening sensation set in. Assuming it was just a compressed nerve, I settled back down to sleep. However, just a few more hours into the night, I woke up again, experiencing numbness on my entire right side. My mind was clouded with confusion, but I recall not wanting to disturb my husband's rest, so I mustered the strength to move myself to the den, where I napped until daylight.

That morning I managed to get dressed and go to work despite my mind still being in a haze. However, by noon, it became evident I needed medical attention. The nearest clinic accepting sick calls was an hour away. I drove there using my left arm to steer and my left foot to accelerate and brake because my right side was simply too weak.

That visit marked the beginning of a series of doctor's appointments that unfolded within a span of two weeks. I was diagnosed with multiple sclerosis, commonly known as MS.

I didn't know anything about MS or anyone afflicted by the disease, so I did what was becoming popular—I googled it. And, as was a common tendency, I assumed the worst, convinced I would soon succumb to the effects of the disease and die.

That was over eighteen years ago.

I didn't die, but my idea of what life should be did. Every other-than-work activity I was involved in stopped except for caring for my mother, from whom I hid my condition because she was too frail at the time.

It soon became apparent that I could no longer continue working either. MS had affected my long- and short-term memory, making me a liability to the company. My once-obsessive chase for fulfillment transformed into a complete detachment from society and all my life goals.

I was utterly lost. Overwhelmed by grief and confusion, I found myself on the floor in the corner of the guest bedroom one day. I curled into a fetal position and cried uncontrollably. In anger, I decided to confront God: "God, I was trying to be the perfect wife, mother, and daughter. I was building my career and helping others. I was working in church—Your church! And look what You've allowed."

It wasn't reverent. But it was genuine.

God chose to answer me immediately. If anyone had been in the room, they wouldn't have heard anything. But His answer struck my inner being like a lightning bolt, followed by a rumbling that grew in intensity until His words resonated with every part of my core.

> As each one has received a gift, minister it to one another, as good stewards of the manifold grace of God.
>
> —1 PETER 4:10 (NKJV)

He said, *Every breath you make, every step you take, is from Me and for Me.*

That was it.

God might have offered soft, reassuring, comforting words to someone else. But He knew exactly what was required for my headstrong and determined personality. He knew I would only listen if my life was stripped of all the distractions that accompany the world's definition of success.

I wish I had humbled myself at that moment. But I was still angry, so I defiantly responded, "Fine, You handle it."

Looking back, I envision God arching an eyebrow, much like a loving parent would in response to the antics of a loved but self-centered child. How silly of me to assume He hadn't been handling everything all along.

Surrendering my preconceived idea of what life was supposed to look like was difficult. Burying the notion that I had control of anything went against every grain of my too-assertive personality. However, multiple sclerosis was and still is a constant reminder that my influence over matters is limited.

Recovering from that initial exacerbation, which was triggered by excessive stress, took several years. During the quiet season of healing, I studied the Bible and was often reminded that God had always been in charge and would always have my best interests at heart. I gradually came to understand that my unabated busyness was an assault on God's plan for my peace and security.

> **And God is able to make all grace abound toward you, that you, always having all sufficiency in all things, may have an abundance for every good work.**
>
> —2 CORINTHIANS 9:8 (NKJV)

As my body regained strength, I deliberately adopted a simplified schedule to care for my mother, who had miraculously outlived her cancer. And when the time came for my grandson to face his own battle with cancer, I ensured my plans remained light so that I could help with his challenging journey.

As the MS-induced brain fog lifted, I allowed God to replace it with the concept of grace. I felt His favor settle over me as I acknowledged His perfect timing, enabling me to care for my loved ones while relying on His grace to guide me through the uncertainties.

After all these years, I occasionally want to tell God what's best. That's when Paul's conversation with God comes to mind. He asked the Almighty to remove a thorn in his life: "And He said to me, 'My grace is sufficient for you, for My strength is made perfect in weakness.' Therefore most gladly I will rather boast in my infirmities, that the power of Christ may rest upon me" (2 Corinthians 12:9, NKJV).

God allowed MS in my life to change my plans, leading me to embark on a different path. Ten years after my diagnosis, I was much healthier, and my family members were doing well enough to no longer require my care. So I began The Grace Warrior Ministry. I didn't know what the ministry was to be, what it would look like, or even achieve. I just knew that God wanted me to walk alongside Him as a warrior, spreading the message of His all-sufficient grace.

I am now a writer, speaker, and a certified Christian life coach. Under the banner of The Grace Warrior, I've been blessed with many opportunities to teach, equip, and motivate women. I encourage them to trust God as He lavishes His unmerited favor upon their lives.

I always aim to be the Grace Warrior that God has called me to be, with all that I am and have. As a professional, but above all, as The Grace Warrior, my message to everyone is the same—God's grace is all you need.

As we grow in faith, we wait
in silence. As we listen for
His voice, we have hope that
He will speak. It may not
be a loud boom or thunder,
but a soft whisper.

—Dana Arcuri, author

CHAPTER 2
God's Many Voices

Biscuits

Rachel M. Mathew

We sat around the battered old dining room table, holding
hands, preparing to sing our blessing for the meal. The two-
story frame house in rural northeast Ohio was drafty and cold.
What more could we expect for $5,000 in 1956? Mom was at
one end of the table and Dad at the other, with us three girls
on one side and our three little brothers on the other.

We were a lovely family to look at. Five of us had blond
hair and blue eyes like Dad. Only one brother had brown hair,
like our pretty mother, but even he had blue eyes. My hair was
really curly like Dad's. I looked a lot like him. I got a lot of
attention because of my hair, and even strangers would ask me,
"Where did you get those pretty curls?"

Dad was in charge, like he always was when he was home, and
he somehow managed that without speaking. Whenever Mom
or one of the children wanted seconds we would say, for example,
"Biscuits, please." Dad didn't have to do that. He just looked at
what he wanted and we were expected to pass it to him.

Mom and Dad had married out of mutual attraction with
almost nothing else in common. Neither of them really knew
at the time that Dad was already an alcoholic, but they soon
found out—and so did we as soon as we became old enough.
Mom didn't hold back about sharing adult concerns with us.
When Dad was sober, he worked hard and came home at

night, but he rarely spoke. When he was drinking, he was totally unpredictable and sometimes violent. He would often just disappear from home and from his job. He was an excellent auto mechanic, but we could never get ahead, and when he missed paychecks it led to bad times at home. We might come home to a cold house because there was no coal for the furnace. Sometimes we had no electricity or phone service. We never knew what to expect. He was home that night after having worked all day. He sat silently there in his grease-stained work clothes, cigarettes in his breast pocket, glaring down at the food.

★★★

My therapist, Maureen, must have seen my tension rise as I got to this part of the story. I went silent, hands clenched in my lap and staring at the floor.

I had decided to go into therapy after reading Charles Sheldon's classic book *In His Steps*. The question in the book, "What would Jesus do?", led me to pray and think about what I needed to start or stop doing. It seemed to me that God wanted me to seek help and healing from my childhood traumas. So, at the age of forty-five, I was finally taking steps to work through the lifelong anxiety that drove me to constantly try to please others.

> **Cast all your anxiety on Him, because He cares about you.**
>
> —1 PETER 5:7 (NASB)

"Can you give your anxiety to Jesus to hold while we do this?" Maureen murmured. "That way it won't interfere with this process."

"Oh no," I blurted out. "I love Jesus! I don't want Him to feel this!"

I carried on, forcing myself to relive the memory.

***

That meal was a big deal to me because I had made the whole thing by myself. Each of us girls was expected to take our turn cooking. My older sisters, Jeanne and Becky, had their turn when they were younger, and now that they were older they were involved in all sorts of after-school extracurricular activities. I was twelve years old when my turn came. We had no convenience foods, no boxed mixes. Everything was made from scratch. The standard meal was meat, potatoes, vegetable, and hot bread. But all I remember making that day is the biscuits. I had seen Mom make them one way

> **Blessed be the God and Father of our Lord Jesus Christ, the Father of mercies and God of all comfort.**
>
> **—2 CORINTHIANS 1:3 (NASB)**

and Grandma make them another way. I knew the recipe by heart, but hadn't had anyone watch me make them or guide me in how to handle the dough. I somehow managed to mix the stiff dough, roll it out, and then cut the biscuits out into neat round circles. I popped them into a 400-degree oven and left them in until the last minute so they could be served piping hot. The hungry family was waiting impatiently when I finally carried them to the table, just like a grown woman. I still had on my apron covered in flour. My head was high. I had done it all myself.

After the blessings, we all helped ourselves to the dish in front of us. As I picked up my fork, a biscuit flew down the table and hit the mirror on the far wall behind us with a thud. Everyone jumped and then turned toward the end of the table where Dad sat. He started shouting at Mom in a fury.

"I had to suffer through your biscuits! I had to suffer through Jeanne's biscuits! I had to suffer through Becky's biscuits! And now—"

That's all I remember of what he said, but I filled in the rest of his incomplete sentence in my head. Now he was being subjected to my biscuits and they were horrible! Our normally silent father was furious, and it was my fault because my biscuits were no good.

I froze, with my fork in place, stunned and afraid to move. Inside, I collapsed emotionally in mute agony. I felt heat on my face and knew it must be bright red. Was there a spotlight on me? Tears dripped into a sticky paste on the floured apron covering my lap.

★★★

"That's the kind of experience I grew up with," I told Maureen. "By the time I was an adult, it just became a habit for me to watch others, trying to anticipate what they wanted, and trying to please them. Sometimes I'd even give them things they hadn't asked for and didn't have a right to."

We talked about that for a bit. "When did you accept Christ?" she asked.

"When I was eight years old. I've spent a lot of time since then reading and studying the Bible, but when I do, I search for ways to please Him and avoid His displeasure. Every time I hear my pastor call Him Father, I get a pit in my stomach." *I can't imagine dumping my anxiety on Jesus*, I added in my thoughts, remembering Maureen's suggestion.

That was the moment. For the first time ever, in that therapy session, I heard Him speak directly to me!

That's what a Savior is for.

I was shocked. The voice was in my mind, not out loud, and I don't know how I knew it was Jesus, but I was certain it was. If I had tried to imagine what Jesus would say to me if He was there, it would have been something like, "Shame on you for feeling sorry for yourself!" But that wasn't it at all.

> # For my father and my mother have forsaken me, but the LORD will take me up.
>
> —PSALM 27:10 (NASB)

I understood immediately what He meant with those beautiful and exquisite words. I felt His love flood over me. His love was so great that He wanted to take my anxiety on Himself!

That was a real turning point for me, both in my faith and in my life. Now instead of imagining Jesus as an angry, volatile father who might lash out at any moment, I can easily imagine Him sitting at the table with us eating one of those biscuits, as imperfectly made as they were, just like the perfect Daddy He is. I can even picture Him struggling to swallow the dry bread stuck to the roof of His mouth, with crumbs on His beard. He looks at me with delight in His twinkling eyes and says, "Mmm, good! Thank you so much for making Me these biscuits, daughter!"

GOD'S GIFT OF SMELL
— Heidi Gaul —

THE YEASTY FRAGRANCE of bread as it bakes. The "new car" air freshener hanging from a rearview mirror. A gardenia in bloom. How can one simple scent conjure up so many memories? The olfactory system links directly to the two specific parts of the brain connected with emotion and memory. None of the other senses do. Because of this, memories triggered by the sense of smell are older and more vivid than those attached to our other senses. Our noses do more than distinguish one fragrance from another—they take us back in time!

In the years following that fateful dinner, I learned to make better biscuits. With the help of a kind friend, I learned the secret to working with the dough, and I'm told that now they're pretty awesome! Even better, I've learned to make peace with myself—and my father. Late in his life, my father was able to gain and maintain sobriety. We were blessed to have a loving relationship with lots of pleasant conversations during the last ten years of his life. But more than that, I've been blessed with a strong relationship with my heavenly Father, who came to me in my time of need and let me see His infinite love.

His Redeeming Voice

Kris Sheppa

It was 1972. Richard M. Nixon was our thirty-seventh president.
A gallon of gas cost just thirty-six cents, the Dallas Cowboys had
won the Super Bowl. We all watched M★A★S★H, *All in the Family*,
and *The Waltons* on TV while we ate Jiffy Pop popcorn. My
favorite jeans were bell bottoms, and my hair was long and straight.
To say that I had deep-rooted hippie genes would be an under-
statement. If I had been old enough in 1969, I would have been at
Woodstock. As it was, I had to experience it in a movie theatre.

My divorced mother had her hands full raising three teenagers on her own. She worked long hours as a registered nurse, so
I did not see her much. It was not until years later that I found
out it was her unwavering faith in God that got her through
her difficult life.

I myself had given up on God. My father left us when I
was only six years old, and my mother struggled her whole
life to keep us all fed and clothed with never a helping hand
from him. As a young girl I saw a lot of hurt and conflict never
resolved, and I always thought of God as neglectful and distant,
pretty much like my own father had been.

My mother tried hard to teach us about God and His
unconditional love. I remember many Sundays how she would
coax and bribe us to go to church, and she made sure that we
went to Sunday school and catechism classes. But I never felt

any sense of belonging or connection to God. I just figured that God did not exist, or if He did, then He did not care about me or anyone else.

Drugs became a big part of my life during my teenage years. When I was only 11 years old, I smoked my first joint, and immediately I was hooked. By the time I was 13, I had begun experimenting with LSD and other drugs. In those days it was like drinking water—I was given a never-ending supply by the people I knew, so I naturally fell into this habit. Most of my days and nights were spent on a continual high.

I began to skip school a lot, and when I did show up, I would spend much of my time in the principal's office, usually because of my disrespect toward my teachers or some other form of unacceptable

> **You LORD, took up my case; you redeemed my life.**
>
> —LAMENTATIONS 3:58 (NIV)

behavior. My poor mother would have to leave work to come pick me up and then apologize for my unruly behavior to teachers and school officials. I found myself acting up just to get some kind of response from her. But no matter what I did, she only sighed and pleaded for me to try harder. I did not, of course. My disrespect and rebelliousness only got worse.

I soon found myself searching satanic history and rituals in books and other avenues. I began spending more and more time learning occult practices, until it became almost an obsession for me. I was fascinated and deceived. Between the drugs and the satanism, I was truly on a downward and dangerous spiral.

It was 1972, and I was a wild and free-spirited 15-year-old girl until the night everything changed. I had been on a 2-day high, and I fell into a deep sleep. I dreamed I was on a ladder reaching toward heaven. On this ladder were many people of all ages climbing upward. My brother was also on this ladder. Some people were falling off and some were continuing to climb higher. The sky was bright and a beautiful shade of blue above me, while underneath was a dark and dismal pit. As I reached a certain point, I found myself falling, falling ever so slowly. I looked up and noticed that my brother was still climbing higher.

> **Let the redeemed of the LORD tell their story—those He redeemed from the hand of the foe.**
>
> —PSALM 107:2 (NIV)

As I fell, I heard a voice call from heaven. I knew it was God. He spoke directly to me, telling me that I would be lost forever, and that I was about to die physically and spiritually if I did not change my ways.

I woke up shaking and in a cold sweat. I felt that somehow my heart had been changed and my eyes were opened. I could not explain it. It was something I have never forgotten.

My life didn't change a whole lot at first. I didn't tell anyone about the dream, but I began to notice that God kept bringing people into my life who were believers. It seemed that everywhere I went, someone would say something about God's love and forgiveness. After a while I realized that I could not just chalk it up as a coincidence. There was definitely something else going on. I noticed my addiction to drugs was lessening. My fascination with the occult had all but disappeared.

Six months later I met my future husband, Bryan. I had seen him around town before, but I had never paid much attention to him. He came from a completely different background than I did, and he did not fit into my image of what I wanted in a boyfriend: someone rebellious and wild, someone who listened to rock music—someone like me. Bryan was more of a country-music person, relaxed and down to earth. He was different, so different than what I was used to. I felt drawn to him. Looking back, I see God's hand in all of this.

After about a month of spending most of my time with him, he took me to meet his sister. Unbeknownst to me, they had planned to take me to church with them that weekend. Sitting in the pew, my heart was on fire during the whole service, I felt the Holy Spirit not just nudging me, but actually pushing me. At the end of the church service, the pastor asked for those who needed prayer to come forward. I thought that my heart would jump right out of my chest as I grabbed Bryan's hand and led him down the aisle behind me. On our knees that day, together we gave our hearts and our lives to Jesus Christ. Jesus became my Lord and Savior, and I have been in love with Him ever since. And my brother—the one I had dreamed about climbing the ladder—also came to know Jesus Christ as his Savior about 3 years after that. He is still walking with Him to this day.

To say that my life has been changed because of that dream, because of God's grace and intervention, would be an under-statement. I really had no clue as to how amazing, loving, patient, and forgiving our Almighty Father is. I am so grateful that He chose to reach down from heaven and save a young wild child like me. I will forever sing His praises.

The Rainbow Tree

Denise Margaret Ackerman

I may not be your typical Granny. I love to drive my flashy yellow four-wheeler (ATV) through the wooded trails and over the rolling fields on our property. If there are grandchildren visiting, requests for ATV rides with Granny (who drives a bit faster than Pop) are common.

One crisp spring afternoon, the snow had finally melted enough to drive through the wooded trails. Our four-year-old grandson, Daniel, and I bundled up in warm hats and gloves to take our first ride of the season. Daniel had been going through some tough medical issues, but he seemed recovered enough to ride with me. With him snuggled close behind me, his little arms wrapped tightly around my waist, we drove over the ice-covered creek. Up ahead on the trail I noticed a tall cherry tree, bent over from the weight of a winter ice storm. The tree formed a rainbow-shaped arch over the trail. God nudged my heart to stop beneath the arch to talk with Dan.

I stopped the ATV and turned around on my seat to face him. Looking into his deep brown eyes, I asked, "Do you remember the Bible story we read about Noah's ark and the flood that covered the whole earth? After the waters dried up, Noah gave thanks to God for bringing him and his family safely through the flood. Then God put a beautiful rainbow in the sky as a promise that he'd never destroy the earth again like that."

Dan nodded. I pointed to the cherry tree and said, "See the way this tree is bent over like a rainbow? This seems like a good place to talk to God. Is there anything you'd like to thank Him for, buddy?"

Folding his hands, Dan bowed his head and whispered thanks to God for his mommy and daddy, our nice day, and that he was feeling better. My heart melted with the beauty of this exchange between the Lord of the universe and my innocent grandboy.

★★★

Dan has endured more suffering than most little boys. In the months leading up to his second birthday, he began to experience unexplained nosebleeds, recurring respiratory illnesses, and an unnerving pallor to his skin, leading to many appointments as doctors worked to diagnose what was going on.

One Thursday evening, as I was rehearsing Christmas music with our worship team, my cell phone rang. A quick peek showed it was my husband calling. Dan's parents had taken him back to his pediatrician for blood work earlier that day and had promised to let us know how the appointment went.

"Danny is in the hospital." My husband's voice quavered as he relayed the news. "He has leukemia."

Even though I suspected something was terribly wrong with Dan's health, I will never forget the shock I felt when I heard the heartbreaking diagnosis. Putting away my phone, I began to gather my music book and belongings, but my emotions overtook me. I stood there, frozen—my mind flooded with fears over what the outcome might be. Overwhelmed, my feelings of panic began to spill over with tears. One of the team members hugged me as I wept uncontrollably. The entire worship team gathered around me. They prayed for my precious little grandson, placing him in God's care and seeking His presence for each member of my family.

Still blinded by tears, I prayed nonstop as I traveled over slippery, snow-covered roads to get home, where my husband was waiting with Benjamin, Dan's five-year-old brother.

Our family's lives radically changed. Over the next three-and-a-half years that Dan received chemotherapy treatments, Ben spent a lot of time at our home. As grandparents, we were blessed to witness the love and concern that he displayed for his younger brother. If Dan had to fast before a treatment, his brother and parents fasted with him. When Dan had to spend nights in the hospital, Ben would have trouble falling asleep. On one of those sleep-challenged evenings, as I rubbed his back, we used the alphabet to list things we were thankful for: *A* is for animals, *B* is for brother, *C* is for candy, and so on. Eventually, the worried older brother drifted off to sleep.

> **And he took the children in his arms, placed his hands on them and blessed them.**
>
> **—MARK 10:16 (NIV)**

The upheaval in our adult lives was challenging, but it was hard to imagine how a sick child could deal with all this trauma. To reduce Dan's exposure to other children's germs at the babysitter's house, his dad began to work from home. Difficult medical terms like induction, remission, and infusion were spoken as fluently as teddy bear, sippy cup, and blankie. Medications were administered, tracked by complicated schedules.

His parents learned how to flush his port with heparin before inserting chemo drugs into the IV tube. When his mom ran out of sick days at work, I used my own paid time off and then requested unpaid leave. There were many ups and downs: frightening reactions to treatments, hospital stays due to illnesses that depleted Dan's resistance, and numerous painful spinal punctures. All of us who loved him felt our share of anxiety and offered countless prayers for his health. Yet even when Dan was old enough to talk, he never complained about his ongoing painful ordeal.

***

Over the remaining years of his treatment—until he was declared cancer-free at the age of six—and to this day, the rainbow tree has continued to be a treasured place for Dan to talk to God about things that are on his mind. Pausing there in our secluded hideaway, our personal conversations with the Lord are safely kept by the surrounding trees, ferns, and wildlife. As we draw closer to God and one another, we can forget the outside world for a time. Dan prays for his family and thanks God for the simple blessings in his life. Listening to his prayers helps me to better know how I can pray for him. And

> **Let us then approach God's throne of grace with confidence, so that we may receive mercy and find grace to help us in our time of need.**
>
> **—HEBREWS 4:16 (NIV)**

GOD'S GIFT OF SIGHT
— Heidi Gaul —

ALTHOUGH GOD HAS gifted many of us with perfect sight, with His help, modern medicine delivers the miracle of sight to those who have poor vision. For some, a precisely cut lens makes better vision possible. For others, surgery can often provide the ability to see clearly. My eyes were severely nearsighted, and I depended on corrective lenses until my surgery. I cried the first time I saw green leaves without the aid of glasses—individual, magnificent, and on a tree, no less—and counted it a miracle. It was as if I'd been released from a world of darkness into the light.

Although God gave us eyes to see, as our Savior and the Light of the World, Jesus turned our darkness to light.

---

as he hears me pray, he learns about the many times that God has been faithful in my life.

Dan recently celebrated his eleventh birthday. He is a fifth-grade student who loves playing soccer and shooting baskets with his big brother. His vibrant life is a testimony of God's grace. Even though he is now a "tween," Dan continues to enjoy ATV rides with his granny and spending time in God's presence. Our special sanctuary on the trail is the perfect place to seek God, share answered prayers and reflect on how great the Lord is. Dan's sweet faith, embodied in a simple prayer of thanks, inspires my own walk with the Lord—one that renews each time we meet with God beneath our rainbow tree.

God's Heavy Equipment

Janet Laird Mullen

I survey the piano room. It is littered with the things my husband did not want—books and collectibles from 27 years together. A quilt that was a wedding present lays abandoned on the floor; it has served its purpose in covering a family heirloom that has now moved to my husband's new house. The weight of what I have lost sweeps over me, and I decide to take a break from the mess. I strap the leash on Emma, my terrier and now sole companion, and walk across the street to my father-in-law's house. He moved to our town 6 years ago to be closer to us. He was an English teacher, as I am, so we have had a special connection since we first met so many years ago. Before I go in to see him, I stop to survey the work that has begun in his back yard.

A front loader, an impressive track vehicle, and a half-dozen young, strong men armed with chain saws and handsaws cluster around the drainage ditch in my father-in-law's backyard. The ditch is massive, running a half mile along the back property of eight homes. The neighborhood's aging drainage system was put under stress from increased development, and the city was slow to respond. As a result, the concrete structure collapsed in places, causing blockage and flooding. The original damaged zone has eroded to become a ditch 7 feet deep and 10 feet wide, littered with the detritus of many years of poor drainage. There are broken tree limbs, trash, junk neighbors have dumped in it, even a colorful beach ball that floated downstream during a particularly heavy downpour. Today the work is being accomplished with speed and efficiency; it contrasts sharply with the months of waiting and delays that preceded it.

It is late June, and these capable young men are making room for a new ditch, an open system that everyone hopes will solve the current problems. The massive track vehicle digs around long-standing power poles. The buzz of the chain saws quickens my senses: things are happening!

Surveying the ditch, painful thoughts again flood my mind as I think of my own failed system—a 27-year marriage I wanted to preserve, but my husband did not. We once had a deep friendship and a trusting relationship. We supported and encouraged each other; we shared inside jokes and fun adventures. We had poured love and attention into our family. I thought that we would always be together. I never imagined that I would be facing life on my own as a divorced woman. The loss of that primary relationship in my life has left a void. Waves of loneliness still engulf me at unexpected moments, despite my best efforts to be strong. Moving forward is difficult.

> **Behold, I am doing a new thing: now it springs forth, do you not perceive it? I will make a way in the wilderness and rivers in the desert.**
>
> —ISAIAH 43:19 (RSV)

Emma tugs on the leash, interrupting my thoughts. She is eager to walk on. I turn my thoughts back to the present and head in to visit with my father-in-law.

The next day, Emma and I return to my father-in-law's yard to see what has been accomplished. The site around the ditch is bare. Trees that stood in the way of progress have been removed. Power poles have been relocated to accommodate the space needed for the new ditch. Signs of change are unmistakable. Stage one is complete.

And then the work ceases. The equipment is removed. The men do not return. We had hoped and expected for the second stage of the work to immediately follow the first. But as we watch and wait for the next contracted service to come, we are daily disappointed. There is no word from the city about when the work will continue.

Seven weeks later, the work is still at a standstill. Autumn is at hand, and the poison ivy vines climbing along the walls of the ditch are now turning yellow. A lone power pole with tangled wiring still lays on the ground in my father-in-law's backyard, waiting to be carried away. Grass has grown up around it where the mower cannot reach. The old, broken concrete in the ditch remains.

Each day Emma and I walk past my father-in-law's property. We pause, and Emma sniffs the ground for new scents. I stand and look for signs of further progress. But there is nothing. Stage two is delayed. I know my father-in-law is exasperated by the holdup.

I consider the slow progress in my own life. I wonder why certain habits are hard to break. Each day I wake up replaying the events of the last two years of my marriage, trying to make sense of things. I remind myself to let go and move forward; I try to follow the advice given by so many well-meaning friends. Yet it is hard to move forward when healing is not complete, when so many important matters remain unresolved.

The divorce is not final. The waiting continues. So many major life decisions still lay ahead of me. Some days it seems as if my future is a long way off.

Emma pulls me forward on the leash, always wanting to keep moving. As we continue through the neighborhood, I contemplate the nature of progress. My father-in-law's very real mess has begun to be resolved by heavy equipment and trained professionals. The waiting, the stalling, the temporary cessation of activity that he has experienced are part of the process. The contract for the project still stands. The funding is secured. The work has begun. And I have no doubt that at some time in the near future, water will again flow freely along the back of my father-in-law's property. We are between stages, and it is simply time to wait again, which is often not at all simple.

> **For I am confident of this very thing, that He who began a good work among you will complete it by the day of Christ Jesus.**
>
> **—PHILIPPIANS 1:6 (NASB)**

John Milton wrote a beautiful poem that includes these words: "They also serve who only stand and wait." This statement used to perplex me, and I wondered, *How can anyone serve by standing still? By simply waiting? Doesn't serving in its most basic form involve action?*

This long haul in my life is revealing to me the wisdom of Milton's words. God is transforming me through my painful loss. I am daily rising to seek His face, rather than to seek acceptance from others. I am learning to follow His way, not my own. I am finding my joy, my purpose, and my life in Him. And I am seeing that the simplicity of my prayerful and trusting reliance on my God is an act of service to Him. And to others. It silently says, "I trust that You are enough. Only You." Waiting is not inaction; it is trustful expectation.

I cannot do all the work that is needed in my life—the legal, financial, emotional, relational issues. Some of it is beyond my strength and capabilities. There are some things that are just too heavy a load for me to lift. I must hand those things off to Someone greater, mightier, more able than I am.

Like the ditch contract the city has with its subcontractors, God's covenant with me remains. Despite what things look like on the surface of my life, no matter how bleak some days may seem, the reality is that He loves me and is at work in my life. He will protect me and provide for me and see me through this dark time. He is able. I will choose to believe that His might will again act on my behalf, as it has in the past. He will bring His heavy equipment to remove the broken and eroded pieces of my life and to pour a new edifice for His glory.

The Lord is showing me that while I do have to wait for some things to come to pass, I do not have to wait until there is a full resolution of my circumstances before I move forward in faith with Him. His work in me has begun. My heart was broken; now it isn't. I can apply to my circumstances what I have now—my trust in Him—and serve Him in this place of waiting. Even if I simply stand and wait on Him. I am not waiting on human effort, but on the very might of my God, who I know is willing and able.

A New Home and a New Life with God

Rachel Britton

"We'll live here for ten years, at least," said my husband as he turned the key in the lock. I stepped over the threshold of our new home, walked down the hallway and into the empty rooms. We would rip up the carpet in the dining room and stain the floorboards to bring out the magnificence of this early 1900s house. The laughter of children would echo off the walls as they raced in from school, flung their bags on the floor, and ran into the yard that stretched out at the back of the house.

Six months later a For Sale sign hung by the gate. My dreams shattered.

We'd searched for that house an entire year. Finally settled into a neighborhood of south London, I loved the plump blue wisteria flowers that hung over the front door. A black and white tiled path, typical of the Edwardian and Victorian era, led to the front door and continued in the hallway. All those items checked boxes for what I wanted in a home.

I also had established a solid career. I climbed securely onto the management ladder of the prestigious British Broadcasting Corporation (BBC). They were even paying for me to earn an MBA. Dedicated to my work, I also decided this was the perfect time to start a family.

"I'm pregnant," I blurted out excitedly when my husband called from Massachusetts. He had traveled there for work with his company. He had news for me too.

"They want me to relocate here," he replied.

Silence followed after we exchanged those statements. The positive pregnancy test still sat perched on the edge of the bathroom sink. The phone remained at my ear as I tried to take in the enormity of his news. Although only a few weeks pregnant, nesting instincts invaded my mind and body. I did not want to move.

Although I didn't realize it then, God was preparing and guiding me toward a new life with Him.

Planning for a new baby should be a delight. Instead, my days were filled with dread and uncertainty. A US work visa doesn't always come easily. Month after month we waited to receive news that my husband's application had been accepted. Half of me hoped it wouldn't happen and we'd get to stay in London. The other half of me wanted what was best for our future.

During that time I didn't know whether I was coming or going. I had lunch with my friend at work, who already had two children. From her, I learned the pros and cons of childcare versus having a nanny—as if we were staying put. But at the same time, the little bedroom next door to our room that would have made the perfect nursery stood untouched. Unpacked boxes from our move filled the room instead of it being painted blue, pink, or yellow, and deciding where to put the crib.

"She's content in there," said the midwife as she examined my bulging belly. I knew how my baby felt. Two weeks past my due date, I gave birth to a beautiful baby girl.

Four weeks later, international movers swept through our house like a tsunami.

Then the dreaded day arrived. With my six-week-old baby held tightly in my arms and a one-way ticket to Boston, Massachusetts, clutched in my hand, we parted ways with our life in London. I sobbed my way through security at the airport after a tearful parting with my mother and father, brother and sister.

Spring comes earlier in England than in New England. Daffodils and crocuses poke their buds through the soil in February. Trees blossom and bloom in March. As we drove up the highway from Logan Airport toward the town of Andover, I felt as lifeless as the stark gray trees that lined the highway. I had exchanged my fabulous Edwardian home for a bland hotel room in a business park.

To say I struggled in our new life would be an underestimation. But, when I look back I see God caring for me and glimpses of His love, although at the time I didn't know it.

I still had my loving husband and my little baby girl, even though it felt like I had lost everything else. Then, right next door in the rental complex where we chose to live, I met a woman who had just moved from Australia. Her baby boy was two days older than my daughter. We became firm friends and spent hours each day together. However, even though these relationships helped, they were not enough.

As my husband took the reins in establishing and embracing our new life in America, I mourned what I had lost. I missed my home, friends, family, work—my whole life in London. I desperately wanted to put my little girl into the arms of her great-grandmother. I put my MBA work aside, realizing I would no longer be a career mother. And I reprimanded myself for calling a "diaper" a "nappy" even though it was an understandable mistake. I was hitting rock bottom.

One Sunday afternoon the TV blared with Sunday afternoon football as my husband sat and learned the game. Having just got my daughter to take a nap in her travel cot, I slumped to the floor, weeping silently. Weeks and weeks of heartache poured out in tears that soaked my face. My body and mind strained with silent screams because I couldn't bear the thought of another day. I didn't want to continue with this new life. Who could I turn to in my agony? No one, it seemed, could fully understand my pain, or relieve me from my suffering.

Suddenly, I remembered God.

God had not been a part of my life for a long time. Long hours at the office followed by fun evenings out with work colleagues and friends had squeezed Him out of my life. My husband and I lay in bed on Sunday morning instead of getting up for church. We hung out with friends in the afternoon and prepared for a busy work week ahead in the evening.

> ## Before they call I will answer; while they are still speaking I will hear.
>
> —ISAIAH 65:24 (NIV)

I was brought up in a Christian family. I had made a commitment to Christ in my teenage years. It's not that I had stopped believing in God or His Son. God just didn't fit into my life anymore. The more I left Him out, the more I thought God wouldn't approve of or have time for me.

However, in that moment on my bedroom floor, none of that mattered. I was in deep anguish and desperately needed help.

"God, help me," my heart cried. Instantly I felt a sense of peace sweep through me like a gentle breeze.

God had heard my cry. God had answered my prayer.

The football game blared again from the next-door room. My daughter woke up from her nap. Life continued as if nothing had happened, yet I would soon discover that everything had changed within me. Not long afterward, a woman I barely knew asked, "Would you like to come to church?" To my surprise, I realized I had an eagerness like never before. "Yes," I replied.

"Would you like to study the Bible?" a church member asked. "Yes," I replied with eagerness, greedy for God's Word.

"Would you like to recommit your life to Christ?" I raised my hand.

Life was still hard. I shed many tears for all I loved, missed, and had left behind across the Atlantic Ocean. But now I also cried out and upward to my heavenly Father. I still wanted my old life back. I missed my family and friends, but I was beginning to find joy in being part of God's family.

> **Come to me, all you who are weary and burdened, and I will give you rest.**
>
> —MATTHEW 11:28 (NIV)

Most of all, I learned something significant about God.

He never stopped loving me when I disregarded Him. He never stopped pursuing me when I wandered away from Him. He hemmed me in with His protective presence, and in front He directed my path.

God had not moved me away from all I held close to my heart to teach me a lesson for my waywardness. He had brought about this relocation because He loved me and couldn't bear for me to do life without Him. He wanted to give me a life that was better than the one I had planned and dreamed of for myself. And He wanted me to love Him back.

God had been in the wings with His arms held out wide, waiting for me to turn and take notice of Him. However, I had been distracted by all that glittered in life. With the glitter out of the way, God had finally got my attention. When I turned to Him, He eagerly and lovingly swept me up in His arms, answering my cry for help.

There are still days when I miss life in London, but I am no longer a woman without a home. Faith has given me a home with my heavenly Father.

The Lost Dogs

Susan Thogerson Maas

Our family loved our May vacations at the beach—and this year
was no exception. We rented one of several cabins at the Ocean
Locomotion, a motel named after the old caboose that sat out
in the yard. The ocean itself was a short walk through randomly
scattered bleached logs. And the yard contained a large sandpit
that provided a safe place for our young boys, Bryan and Erik, to
play without me having to constantly supervise.

One afternoon I sat on a chair nearby as they dug holes
in the sand and made roads for their toy trucks. I enjoyed just
doing nothing—a rare treat for a mother—and feeling the fresh
ocean breeze on my face. After a bit, the door of the cabin next
to ours opened, and another little boy emerged, plastic pail and
shovel in hand. He was followed by a woman a little younger
than me with long, brown hair. She smiled and walked over.

"Hi, I'm Tracy. And that's my son, David. My husband is out
walking the dogs."

"Mine has gone fishing," I replied. "Nice to meet you."

Tracy sat on a chair next to mine, and we chatted a bit
while the boys played together. Soon my husband, Gary,
returned with a couple of nice trout he caught in a nearby
stream. Tomorrow's breakfast.

"And there come Larry and the dogs," Tracy said, pointing
toward the beach.

The dogs arrived first, galloping madly toward us, ears flapping and tongues out—two black labs and a golden lab. They ran up to Tracy and then to David and our boys, sniffing and licking and dancing around in the sand. All three boys jumped up to play tag with the dogs.

I laughed. "Wish I had that much energy!"

"Me too," Tracy agreed.

Larry eventually corralled the rambunctious dogs and got them into the cabin. I went inside to fix dinner, while the boys continued to play.

A couple of days later, in the early evening, Gary burst through our cabin door.

> Then he calls his friends and neighbors together and says, "Rejoice with me; I have found my lost sheep."
>
> —LUKE 15:6 (NIV)

"Two of the neighbors' dogs ran off," he reported. "I'm going to help look for them."

We all rushed out to see what we could do.

"It's the two black labs," Tracy said, her voice strained. "They chased after a seagull and we lost sight of them. We called and called, but they never came back."

Behind her, her son's lip quivered like he was about ready to cry.

"How can we help?" Gary asked.

"Larry is walking down the beach looking for them," Tracy said. "I wanted to drive around in case they left the beach, but Larry has the car keys in his pocket."

"I'll take our car and check out the side roads around here," Gary volunteered. He got into our car and took off.

"I'd better wait here with David in case the dogs come back on their own," Tracy said. She stared out toward the ocean, frowning.

But what could I do? I felt helpless.

"I'll pray that they return," I said quietly. Would that even do any good? I'd never been that great at prayer, and I had my doubts that God paid much attention to me. But I took Bryan and Erik back inside, and I silently pleaded for the dogs' return.

The sun sank toward the ocean, and darkness began to fall.

> **Praise be to God, who has not rejected my prayer or withheld his love from me!**
>
> —PSALM 66:20 (NIV)

Larry walked up from the beach alone. I went out to hear the news, as he reported to Tracy.

"I followed their footprints as far as I could. They left the beach and headed toward a little lake." He sighed. "I called for them, but they must not have heard."

Tracy frowned. "What more can we do? They could have run for miles."

Later Gary drove into the parking area. By now the boys were in bed, and I walked out to meet him. "Any sign of the dogs?" I asked.

He shook his head. "I drove down every street in the area and circled around the lake, but nothing. Who knows where they've gone? They could be anywhere by now."

The news was discouraging, and yet somehow I felt at peace. I was confident that the dogs would be found. Was that a sign from God or just the hope I wanted to hold on to?

Darkness had settled in by now. Only the moon shone its pale light onto the waves beyond the sand. Tracy said she

GOD'S GIFT OF TOUCH
— Lynne Hartke —

WHETHER OUR PETS are covered with the long hair of a sheep-dog, the curly coat of a poodle, or the short fur of a dachshund, nothing can hide the bond our dogs have with their humans. In return for the care we give them, a pet can lower a person's blood pressure, reduce stress, and provide companionship. When dogs sense emotional turmoil, they often remind their owners of their presence by nudging their humans with their noses, entering their human's space, and positioning themselves near a hand for petting. God knew the relationship would be mutually beneficial to both sides.

wanted to take one more walk down to the beach. She made her way toward the ocean with a small flashlight, while the rest of us returned to our cabins. I continued to silently pray.

Maybe half an hour later we heard someone pounding on our door. My heart leaped. Was the news good or bad? We jerked the door open to see Tracy with two black labs prancing around her.

"They came back," she cried. "They finally came back."

The grin on her face was reflected in Gary's and mine.

"What happened?" I asked.

"I went down and sat on an old log on the beach and started calling for them," she said. "I was about to give up. I'd nearly lost hope of ever seeing those dogs again. But then I did something I haven't done for a very long time."

"What was it?"

"I prayed. I don't even know if I believe in God, but I didn't know what else to do. I prayed. Then they came racing to me, soaking wet from the ocean and jumped all over me, licking my face and wagging their tales with all their might."

Joy shone from her face.

"I'm glad they're all right," Gary said.

> When I am in distress, I call to you, because you answer me.
>
> —PSALM 86:7 (NIV)

"Me too," I added. "And glad your prayers were answered."

Tracy laughed and leaned down to pet the dogs. "I haven't been to church in ten years," she said. "I'm not exactly an atheist, but I have trouble accepting a lot of the Bible." She paused as one dog licked her hand. "However, I may have to rethink my position now."

As I closed the door, I whispered a thank-you to God. Maybe it didn't take an expert in prayer to get God's attention, after all. Just someone willing to acknowledge their need.

God in the Detours

Lori Stanley Roeleveld

I'd always dreamed of serving God through writing. It's my best skill, so it made sense that I hoped to use it to His glory through professional or ministry writing.

When my children were young, I met a man named Les who would eventually become my literary agent. He had discovered my essays in the newspaper, and now he towered over me at a conference offering professional representation.

"It will require intense work, but you have what it takes. Your writing can make a difference for God," he said.

My children's faces appeared in my mind. My husband traveled constantly for work and I'd grown up in a difficult home. I dreamed of writing, but my primary dream was raising a healthy family. I didn't think I had it in me to do both at the same time. Without healthy role models, managing our home and homeschooling required my full focus.

After praying about it, I told the agent my writing dream would have to wait but I'd keep in touch. This decision required a huge investment of faith. I knew I might be parting ways with my writing dream forever.

The year came when my youngest graduated from homeschool. It was a bittersweet time, but I set my sights on the hope I'd entrusted to Jesus until then. I entered a writing contest and won first place. Les became my literary agent, and it seemed my dream of writing full-time for God was about to become reality. My husband, Rob, was on board, and by hanging up my twenty-two-year homeschool teacher hat, I'd now have the time. I had just turned 50, which didn't feel old, exactly, but it did feel like a time to get moving on life's second act.

That's when our family story encountered a major plot twist. My husband's job was suddenly eliminated. We had a mortgage and other bills to pay on top of having two kids in college. We prayed Rob would quickly find work. God had a surprise in store, though. One I didn't like.

> **Trust in the LORD with all your heart, and do not lean on your own understanding. In all your ways acknowledge him, and he will make straight your paths.**
>
> —PROVERBS 3:5–6 (ESV)

I had done some part-time work with families in crisis. Because of a connection there, out of the blue, I was offered a full-time position with benefits in a unique program. Reluctantly, I drove to the interview. This was not the plan. The plan was for me to write full-time, and I believed I had God's blessing on that. Why was I the one with the job offer and not Rob?

During the interview I learned the work was meaningful, I was qualified, and everyone on the panel wanted me to accept. The lead interviewer then told me that others had turned it down. I thought that would be my out until he said they had declined the job *because it required a significant amount of writing*.

In fact, my first responsibility with families would be to write their stories in their voice. In this way, people working with them wouldn't get a list of their problems but would be engaged in the family's values, strengths, culture, faith, and community as well as their needs, all through my writing. I felt God chuckling. I had hopes of writing full-time and He had known just how *full*-time that would be!

For ten years I worked that job by day and wrote blog posts, articles, and books by night. While the writing I did for the day job was often seen only by a handful of people, God used it to change lives. Judges, teachers, state workers, and even the families themselves found renewed hope when they had a fuller picture of the family than just their current crisis. I had initially dreamed of writing bestsellers, but nothing beats knowing a family's life was turned around for good by a single story.

I now shared God's laughter at His unexpected planning. And I was doubly grateful that I had this work when, a couple years later, Rob was diagnosed with multiple sclerosis. He was able to resume carpentry eventually, but during the time when initial symptoms were emerging, medical appointments and tests consumed his days. God always knows the road ahead better than we do.

After 10 years, reliant now on the income, I imagined I would eventually retire from that job. I'd worked with hundreds of families and knew I'd made a positive impact on our community. Still, as I got older, the stress of dealing daily with intense issues like domestic violence, child abuse, drug addiction, and even trafficking took a toll on my heart, soul, and body. My doctor urged me to cut back on something—but how could I?

Several months later, another detour sign blocked our expected path. Through unforeseen circumstances, my day job was suddenly, jarringly eliminated. At sixty-one, I was officially unemployed.

I imagine God shook His head at the irony that I now cried out to Him about the loss of a job I hadn't initially wanted to take. It was true that I'd prayed to not have to do that work and to be free to minister full-time, but now I could not see where the provision was and felt ill-equipped to make it come about.

As I prayed, though, I had a growing sense of peace. I had been studying about the Israelites and their deliverance from Egypt. They had long prayed for freedom, but I imagine when it came, it was also jarring and unexpected (and a little frightening being chased by Pharaoh's army). I became convicted that as unplanned as this job loss was, God intended it for my good and for His glory.

> **Delight yourself in the LORD, and he will give you the desires of your heart.**
>
> —PSALM 37:4 (ESV)

That's when I asked God to confirm this unexpected detour was part of His plan to take me out of the Egypt of that demanding job and into my promised land of full-time ministry through words. For the first night in a week, I slept well.

The next morning I heard my phone announce a text. Once I was awake and had completed my time with the Lord, I opened it. One of the lovely couples who pray for my writing ministry had been discussing my job loss with God before I even woke that day. They wrote: "As we've prayed for you this morning, it came to us that God is taking you out of your

Egypt and into your promised land. Does that mean anything to you?"

It certainly did.

I couldn't even type a response. Tearfully, I fell to my knees and thanked God for His presence and provision during all the detours of life. I like certainty and safe plans, but God has helped me learn to trust Him in every circumstance. I had a new appreciation for what the Israelites faced in the wilderness because I knew nothing about being self-employed. But I believed God would be there to guide and provide just as He has been through all these years.

My first agent, Les, is retired now, but I'll never forget the things he taught me. The morning after my first-place win all those years ago, Les sat down with me at the conference breakfast for a chat.

"Winning is very fun," he said, smiling.

I agreed.

Then he got serious. "Listen now, you're heading home today where there won't be applause, ribbons, or plaques, just God, and the work, and the words. The writing journey has many detours, but God is with you always. Keep your eyes on Him and work, every day, for what has eternal worth."

God has provided me with a life I couldn't have imagined and would never have known to ask for in prayer. His dreams for me are greater than my own, and they encompass every twist, turn, and detour along the way.

The meeting of two
personalities is like the contact
of two chemical substances:
if there is any reaction, both
are transformed.

—Carl Jung

CHAPTER 3

Divinely Orchestrated Encounters

God, Healing, and That Blasted Cat

Julie Lavender

"Here, kitty, kitty, kitty." I raised my voice a couple of octaves and started pleading before shutting the car door.

"Come here, kitty, kitty." I kept calling while I plunged my head in the trunk to retrieve the bag of dry cat food. *Where is that blasted cat? Doesn't he know I'm in a hurry to get to the hospital and check on Mama?*

"Meow." I heard him first, then watched as Snowflake darted up the dilapidated wheelchair ramp while I climbed the three stairs on the other side of the deck. Snowflake halted, like always, just out of reach, and waited for me to pour food into the bowl. No amount of coaxing brought the feline any closer. Which didn't really matter—I didn't like him any more than he liked me. In fact, I was pretty sure only two people liked him, God and my mom.

Snowflake had showed up at my parents' double-wide trailer about five years ago, a mangy-looking stray with ribs protruding like slats on our old barn.

Mama loves any of God's critters, but she seems to have a special place in her heart for the downtrodden or unlovable ones. For the last five years, Mama provided a good life for Snowflake, even though he didn't return the affection. No matter how hard she tried, she just couldn't get the "wild" out of him. After many months, Snowflake let Mama pet him—but only her—as long as she didn't make any sudden movements. He wandered the eighty-five-acre farm, showing up for feedings, but refused domestication. Snowflake received much from Mama and never gave in return. Yet she loved him unconditionally.

Snowflake was the reason I'd been showing up at Mama's empty double-wide twice a day for the last six weeks. Mama had moved into a brick home in a neighborhood summer before last. It took some time to convince her to leave the farm after Daddy died, and even though we'd finally persuaded her to move, she feared that if she trapped Snowflake and took him to her new home, he would run away, never to be seen again. So she made the trip to feed him, twice a day, every day. Personally, I think she used it as an excuse to visit her memories.

The entire property seemed lonely and abandoned. Just like I felt. *God, where are You? Why aren't You healing Mama?*

Mama's daily trips to feed Snowflake stopped abruptly in the fall, eight weeks ago. I'd taken Mama to our local hospital to check a bile duct cyst that doctors had been monitoring since before Daddy passed away. It was a routine procedure—until the physician accidentally punctured her bile duct. Caustic

> He says, "Be still, and know that I am God; I will be exalted among the nations, I will be exalted in the earth."
>
> —PSALM 46:10 (NIV)

bile leaked onto some of her internal organs, causing excruciating pain.

I prayed often, but most of the time my prayers were just whispers. "Jesus. Jesus." Diagnoses and prognoses changed hourly. The only thing that remained constant were the daily trips back and forth to feed the cat, a job I took over from Mama. When it was my turn to stay with Mama, one of my kids fed Snowflake.

> **Be strong and courageous. Do not be afraid or terrified because of them, for the LORD your God goes with you; he will never leave you nor forsake you.**
>
> —DEUTERONOMY 31:6 (NIV)

Each time I stopped by to feed Snowflake, I needed visual confirmation that he was OK. There was an urgency about keeping him alive and healthy; some part of me felt as if Mama's life depended on him still being there. Yet however faithfully I fed Snowflake, Mama's healing seemed out of reach.

Out of reach—just like Snowflake. I was angry at God for not healing Mama, for abandoning me, just like I was angry at this blasted cat for keeping his distance when I was working so hard to keep him alive.

God, how much more can she take? Please do something!

God, please—where are You?

"Meow." I stole a glance at Snowflake from my position on the deck, where I'd taken just a moment to sit and ponder my mom's condition. *Wait—he's not stopping at his bowl this time. Is he actually walking toward me?*

GOD'S GIFT OF TOUCH
— Tez Brooks —

WHETHER ROSE PETALS or kittens, sandpaper, or hot coals—the Creator wanted humankind to experience His creation intricately. So, the skin contains several types of touch receptors. Some parts of the body have more receptors than others. For instance, fingers are more sensitive than the shoulders and back. When touching something (hot, cold, pain, or pressure), the touch receptors speed information to the brain. The brain receives the signal and reports how something feels, so the person knows to pull away or pause and enjoy the sensation. The sense of touch is a precious but underappreciated gift from God.

I sat very still. I didn't want to startle him with a sudden movement. Slowly and cautiously, Snowflake approached and gently brushed against my jean-clad leg. I lifted one hand and gingerly touched his back. He didn't bristle nor scamper.

Be still.

I rubbed his ears. I ran my hand across his furry white back. He arched to meet my fingers. "Meow." He brushed against my leg again, but bumped the food bag. The noise frightened him and he shot back to his bowl, stopping to nibble on the bits of food.

Watching Snowflake thrust his head for another bite, I thought about how God had taken care of this antisocial feline. And if God could take care of Snowflake, couldn't He take care of my mom, a kindhearted woman who was loved by many? In

> **If you love those who love you, what credit is that to you? Even sinners love those who love them.**
>
> —LUKE 6:32 (NIV)

fact, hadn't He been doing so all along? God hadn't been unreachable at all; I was just too frightened and busy to feel His presence, to notice. All I needed was to be still long enough to realize that.

Thank You, God. For taking care of Mama. For hanging on to me. For loving this blasted cat.

Maybe God and healing—and my appreciation for Snowflake—weren't quite so out of reach after all.

Unlocked Faith

Shannon Leach

I sat slumped on the couch, staring at the tiny TV as the tears
I had spent the last twenty minutes fighting back fell on my
worn high-school T-shirt. I shamed myself for being so weak.
I knew this holiday was coming and knew I would hate it. In
fact, I had made a pact with myself to ignore it completely. As
long as I didn't acknowledge the celebrations of Thanksgiving
that had been popping up around me all week like a jack-in-
the-box with a broken latch, I did not have to acknowledge that
I was anything but thankful.

Except that this holiday was everywhere. I had been battling
rising anxiety since the first decorations of fall had appeared
on the front doors of what seemed like every neighbor on
my street. Turning on the TV had been a bad idea. Thanksgiving something on every channel mocked me. The parade
had seemed like a safe choice, but not even the distraction of
watching balloon handlers fight gale-force winds could stop
the sadness.

I looked around the barren room, blank spaces reminding
me of what had been. Getting married right out of high school
had sounded like such a great idea. Especially for a retired foster
kid who had no idea what to do after the state handed over
independence and loneliness as an eighteenth birthday gift.
I am sure subconsciously it was my way of building the one

thing I had always wished for—a family who loved me and a place where I belonged. But it turned out I could not build a family or a marriage on lies. Not the ones I was told, or the ones I told myself.

My foster mom had tried to comfort me when she found out about the divorce. But her constant talk of God this and Jesus that didn't help anything. If God was so great, then where had He been all this time? Why was I signing divorce papers at 21 years old and working at a gas station while I fought my way through school, surviving on student loans? Why was I sitting here alone, wallowing in heartache and misery while everyone around me was surrounded by people who loved them? Where was this Jesus now, today, in all this pain?

> **I will not leave you as orphans; I will come to you.**
>
> —JOHN 14:18 (NIV)

I imagined my foster mom sitting around the table with family. She and my foster dad were two of the few humans in the world I trusted. Part of me wanted to get in the car and drive back to the house that had been my only home for several years and eat turkey and pie at that big dining room table as if I belonged there. But I couldn't do that, because I didn't. Even though they never made me feel that way, I knew my place. Part family, part stranger. Today, of all days, I didn't need any more reasons to question whether or not I was wanted.

Obviously, ignoring the holiday wasn't working. Maybe I needed to embrace it instead. I stood in rebellion and paced the floor, trying to think of the most Thanksgiving thing I could do. Pie. Pumpkin pie. I didn't need a family to start that tradition. I could do that all by myself. I grabbed my keys and jacket, locked the door, and stepped out into the crisp, windy fall air. I pulled my jacket tighter as I walked to my new-to-me 10-year-old car, begging under my breath for it to start. It turned over without a pause.

As I parked on the outskirts of the unexpectedly crowded lot, I felt an ache as I saw a smiling couple pass in front of me, carrying handfuls of grocery bags. I tried not to torture myself any further by watching them as I got out and shut the creaky car door. But it was no use. Their cheerful faces haunted me all through the store as I searched for my comfort in the frozen-dessert aisle.

I checked out quickly, walked back to my car, and grabbed the door handle. Locked. I reached into my pocket to get my keys and my hand came out empty. Panic took hold as I looked inside and saw my keys hanging from the ignition. I slid down the side of the car to the ground and put my head in my hands. Could this day get any worse?

My foster mom's voice played in my mind as if on cue. *He will not leave you.* Yeah, right. Where was this Jesus now?

"Are you OK?" asked a familiar voice.

I looked up to see the pastor of a church I had visited a few times over the summer standing before me. I stared at him with red and weary eyes.

"Do you need some help?" he asked.

My words and tears spilled out onto the broken concrete as I described my failed attempt at Thanksgiving. He was patient and kind and offered me a ride to get my spare keys from my house and bring me back to my car. He was somehow conveniently parked right next to me. It was my first thankful yes of the day.

As he navigated my directions back to my house, he said the words I was hoping would not be said.

"So, we are having a big Thanksgiving meal at my house in about an hour. You are welcome to join us if you would like. I was just at the store grabbing some last-minute items."

I thanked him, politely declined, and attempted to shift the conversation to small talk, knowing the last thing I wanted to do right now was become a pity guest at someone's family dinner as they talked about how thankful they were to have one another. We arrived at my house, and I acknowledged my second thankful moment of the day as I fished out the key I had hidden under the mat. I grabbed my spare car keys from inside and hoped the questions on the ride back would remain light despite my parking lot breakdown to someone I barely knew.

> **Peace I leave with you; my peace I give you. I do not give to you as the world gives. Do not let your hearts be troubled and do not be afraid.**
>
> —JOHN 14:27 (NIV)

They did. But as we arrived at my car and I started to get out, he offered me a scrap of paper with something written on it.

"Here's my address, in case you change your mind. The invitation is still open, and we would love to have you," he said with a smile that almost made his eyes twinkle.

I smiled, thanked him again, and waved as he drove away.

Fifteen minutes later, I set the defrosting pumpkin pie on the empty counter in my narrow galley kitchen. As I turned around, my gaze rested on a walnut-framed painting of a man rowing in a canoe alone in the wilderness. The pangs of loneliness returned. I looked back and forth between that painting and that pie, hearing the echo of the word *alone* again and again in my mind. Then, a still, small voice in the silence whispered, *You are not alone.* I listened again. Then, with no understanding of why, I walked down the hall to go put on something that was more presentable for a Thanksgiving meal.

As I pulled up across the street and confirmed the house number on the paper, I took note of the number of cars in the driveway and on the street. *Ugh. Maybe this was a mistake. He obviously has a huge family.* Despite my fears, I continued across the street and up the concrete steps, confirming I had my keys as I knocked. Those same twinkling eyes appeared as the door opened.

As he took my coat, I made a quick scan around the room, trying to not make eye contact with the people who seemed to be in every nook and cranny of this modest home. As I followed him in for "introductions," I commented about the joys of having such a large family.

He paused, turned around to look at me, and smiled. "That's the thing. This is my family, but not in the way you are thinking. These are all people who didn't have anywhere else to go

> **So do not fear, for I am with you; do not be dismayed, for I am your God. I will strengthen you and help you; I will uphold you with my righteous right hand.**
>
> —ISAIAH 41:10 (NIV)

on the holiday, so we decided to eat together. That way, none of us have to eat alone."

I looked around the room in shock as something inside me unlocked. All these people were alone at Thanksgiving? It wasn't just me? I spent the rest of that Thanksgiving Day meeting the people who would become my family over the next two years. A family of believers who reminded me I had never been alone. Not for one second.

When I look back now, I know there were no accidents that day. I know my foster mom was right, that God was with me in my pain, putting the right people in the right places at one of my lowest moments, bringing me one step at a time to the place where I belonged. There were many like me, feeling like strangers in a world full of darkness, heartache, and tragedy, looking for the key to something more. Looking for the reminder that they had never been alone. I finally found my family, and God was the key to it all.

An Unexpected Encounter

Emily Marszalek

Amid a stressful career transition while navigating some unexpected health issues that cloaked me with fatigue, I was feeling mentally, spiritually, and physically depleted. Instead of brimming with excitement and hope about this new chapter of life, I was instead battling feelings of failure and worthlessness.

One afternoon, despite the overwhelming desire to curl up in bed all day, I was determined to complete a few errands. First stop: pharmacy. Second stop: haircut. Third stop: the library on our local university's campus to exchange a few books. After my prescription was picked up and my split ends trimmed, I jetted to campus.

I rarely enjoyed visits to campus. Parking was often a nightmare, and for this directionally challenged individual, navigating through the maze of buildings, students, and zigzagging campus streets left me feeling flustered and disoriented. I was also feeling extremely fatigued from a new medication, so I anticipated that the lengthy jaunt from the parking lot on the outskirts of campus to the library stationed at its center would be draining. Although I was correct in my estimation, on I went, the dry August heat baking my skin the whole trek to the library. Books returned and a fresh new novel in hand, I was eager to return to my car and head home.

On the walk back to my vehicle, I noticed an elderly gentleman approaching on my path. Walking with a cane in one hand and a weathered brown briefcase in the other, he was wearing a black baseball cap with "Vietnam Veteran" stamped across the center. As the daughter of a Vietnam veteran, I had an especially tender heart for those who served in Vietnam and always made a point of recognizing them for their service. I smiled as we approached each other, and he addressed me first.

"Excuse me," he asked, "do you know where the ROTC building is? I'm not too familiar with campus."

"Oh gosh, I'm not very familiar with campus either," I told the man. I had no idea where the ROTC was housed. Despite feeling entirely unequipped to help him, I prodded him for more information. "Which branch of ROTC are you looking for?" I knew from a previous job on campus that the university had at minimum both a Navy ROTC and an Army ROTC, which were housed in separate buildings.

> **Then I heard the voice of the LORD saying, "Whom shall I send? And who will go for us?" And I said, "Here am I. Send me!"**
>
> —ISAIAH 6:8 (NIV)

"Army."

"Hmm. I'm not sure where Army ROTC is located, either, but let's find out," I replied. "I'm Emily."

"Mike. Nice to meet you."

Mike shared that he was seeking to meet with one of the officers who managed the Army ROTC program to help him clear up something related to his service record. I asked a couple of passing students if they knew where the Army ROTC building was. "I think they're over in Memorial Gym," one of them answered. Whipping out her phone, she pulled up a campus map and pointed to the building in question.

"I think I know where that is in relation to the library," I told Mike. "I'll walk with you over there to be sure."

Unfortunately, the building was a long walk away, and walking with the cane, Mike had to take it slow. Fortunately, we enjoyed rich conversation about his time in the service while we walked. Although he wasn't drafted, Mike told me with a chuckle, he had intentionally volunteered toward the end of the war hoping he wouldn't be deployed. His plan didn't work; he was still sent to Vietnam.

We slowly inched our way across campus as the sun beat down on us. As sweat began dripping down my back, I started to become concerned about my new friend. He was wearing long pants and long sleeves, and it would be easy for him to overheat. My concern escalated when Mike told me he had been hospitalized the month prior for heat stroke.

Finally we made it to Memorial Gym. Climbing the steps to the entrance, Mike taking one stair at a time, we entered the unlocked building to find it completely empty: not a person in sight. Mike had thought the ROTC department was on the third floor, but after a thorough search of the third floor, it seemed abandoned. After stumbling upon a sign indicating Army ROTC was now in the basement, we descended several floors to find a complete maze, and an empty one at that. Doors were locked and lights were off everywhere we looked.

Mike and I both were overheated, exhausted, and discouraged. I offered up a silent prayer, feeling helpless in my efforts to help: *God, please help us to find the ROTC department.* Almost immediately after my humble plea, we encountered a young woman typing away on a laptop on a couch in an ill-lit corner of the basement maze.

"Excuse me, is the Army ROTC in this building?" I asked.

The young woman laughed. "Well, I've heard Army ROTC is here, but they must have a secret entrance on the other side of the building, because I've never seen them!" Although I smiled and thanked her for her help, I didn't feel much like smiling.

> **That is why, for Christ's sake, I delight in weaknesses, in insults, in hardships, in persecutions, in difficulties. For when I am weak, then I am strong.**
>
> —2 CORINTHIANS 12:10 (NIV)

"Mike, do you want to take a seat here while I poke around the side of the building to see if I can find anything?" He seemed relieved at the suggestion.

Sweat now fully soaked through my T-shirt, I tramped around the west side of the building to find a sign indicating the entrance for Army ROTC: indeed a secret entrance! The exterior door was unlocked, but all the internal doors to the ROTC department were locked and all the lights off. Forceful knocks on each door were left unanswered. Running back to the front entrance to find Mike patiently waiting inside, I delivered the disappointing news. "I found the ROTC department, but no one is there. They must be off doing summer training. I'm so sorry."

Mike indicated he would try again another day and call ahead to make sure someone would be available to meet with him. After the lengthy venture throughout campus, he just wanted to go home. So did I. As I thought about the long trek back to our parked cars, I was thoroughly concerned for Mike, knowing he was still recovering from heatstroke. I feared he wouldn't be able to endure the walk.

"How about we find you a nice shady spot to sit, I'll go find my car and come back to pick you up and drive you to your car?" Mike agreed that was best.

"But I don't think you can drive your car up here," he said. "The sign says this road is for university vehicles only."

"I'll break the rules for you," I said with a wink.

Leaving Mike resting on a shaded bench, I hustled in the direction I thought I parked my car. No doubt with the Holy Spirit's navigational help, I found my car within fifteen minutes. Circling back to where I had left Mike, I saw he had inched his way toward the main campus road. I guess he didn't want me breaking the rules for him after all.

> **And we know that in all things God works for the good of those who love him, who have been called according to his purpose.**
>
> **—ROMANS 8:28 (NIV)**

"Your curbside service has arrived!" I said as I pulled up and leaned over to open the door for Mike. It took us another twenty minutes to find where Mike had parked. He apologized for being forgetful, noting it was a side effect of the heat stroke. I assured him it was no problem and bashfully admitted that on at least a dozen occasions I had forgotten where I parked. Finally finding his car, he thanked me for my efforts to help him. I told him it was

GOD'S GIFT OF TASTE

— Lynne Hartke —

CACTI ARE WELL-KNOWN for their spiny nature, and those spines can hurt humans and animals. Yet there are a few varieties that offer a culinary delight, including prickly pear. If you can avoid the tiny hairlike spines on the outside of its fruit, you will be rewarded with something that tastes like mild melon. Perhaps God, in His infinite wisdom, designed this cactus to teach us a godly lesson about our worth. 1 Peter 3:3–4 (NIV) says, "Your beauty should not come from outward adornment. . . . Rather, it should be that of your inner self, the unfading beauty of a gentle and quiet spirit, which is of great worth in God's sight." Even the prickliest things can have value.

---

my pleasure and that our conversation had been the highlight of my entire week. Before we departed, I placed a hand on his shoulder and said, "God bless you, Mike."

"God bless you too," he said before gingerly exiting my car and climbing into his own.

As we headed our separate ways, I was overcome with gratitude for the encounter that led to an unexpected blessing and an unexpected new friend. I haven't a doubt God orchestrated our paths to cross that hot afternoon, knowing how much we would need each other in that moment.

Although I had been feeling empty, convinced I had nothing left to offer others, or God, God had used me in my weakness to help and love on a stranger in need. It was a reminder that no matter how broken, empty, or battered we may feel,

God can and will still use us to accomplish His wondrous purposes, if only the cry of our hearts will remain, "Lord, I am willing. Use me." He will strengthen us in our weakness, use us as conduits to share His love with others, and make His mighty presence known.

Opposites Attract

Heather Spiva

I heard her loud voice from across the room.

To be clear, the room was huge: a warehouse space. There were also many other people in the building talking and moving about, yet I could still hear her voice over everything else.

Her voice was large—it was loud, raspy, gravelly, and in no way demure. That is precisely why I noticed her, why I was semi-intrigued—and also hoping to hide from her.

As a vintage clothing reseller, I'm in thrift stores regularly. Other than estate sales, garage sales, word-of-mouth leads, or donations, most of the clothing I find is from thrift stores because there's so much to choose from assembled in one place. It means less work for me.

This woman, though, was messing up my routine. I was perusing the aisles, treasure-hunting if you will, and she insisted on talking to me as we approached each other. I don't mind talking to people, but when I'm thrifting, on my quest out in the wild world of vintage clothing hunting, I'm focused. Taking the time to talk about things I may not want to talk about or to explain why I have what I have in my hands—which seems to happen frequently in thrift stores—wasn't on my agenda. I needed to get through this store and move on to the next one. This is what treasure hunting is all about.

So I was focused, and I didn't have time to chat with any-one…particularly someone who wasn't my style. That sounds rude to say, but isn't that how we think? We tend to mix with similar folks and keep them close to us and those less familiar at arm's length. We gravitate toward like-minded individuals, and if their personality melds with ours, even better.

This lady wasn't my style.

She was confrontational, gregarious, and outgoing to the max—my polar opposite. More than that, I recognized her as someone I'd seen at this thrift store before. That meant that if I began to chat with her now, I'd have to talk to her every time I saw her, further taking me out of my thrifting routine. My focus would be ruined. The introverted me wasn't keen on this. But God always has His plans. And as I

> The LORD does not look at the things people look at. People look at the outward appearance, but the LORD looks at the heart.
>
> —1 SAMUEL 16:7 (NIV)

would find out, His plans are the best—even if we're confused, confounded, or downright stubborn about letting Him have His way.

Much to my dismay, she had found me. She looked at what I was carrying in my hands and proceeded to talk to me about it.

"Ooh, what do you have there? Wow. What a great find. I was just in this area and I didn't see that! My name is Becky. I'm here all the time. Isn't this a great place?" Before I could reply to any of her questions, she had moved on to what she was holding. Her comments were coming fast, she was talking loudly, and I could feel other people looking at us.

I should've crawled away from her. But something strange was happening. I didn't *feel* like getting away. While my defenses were up, and I was ready to cut the conversation short if I needed to, there was something about her that agreed with me. I felt like God was nudging me in the ribs and whispering in my ear, *pursue her, pursue her.*

Looking back later, I tried to pin down what drew me to her. Maybe it was the way she spoke: to the point, offensive at times, but heartfelt. Maybe it was the way her coke-bottle glasses magnified her eyes, giving her an animated, almost cartoonish look. Maybe it was the way she dressed, wearing the most oddly perfect combination of leggings, oversized skirts, jackets, tie-dyed shirts, and uniquely accented costume vintage jewelry. Any of those could have been the reason I used to reject her as a friend, but I was instead compelled to accept her.

> **A friend loves at all times, and a brother is born for a time of adversity.**
>
> —PROVERBS 17:17 (NIV)

After that first conversation, Becky and I began meeting for weekly coffee before the thrift store opened. Without a doubt, our love of vintage—preserving, keeping, and caring for it—is what made us tick as friends. While she doesn't sell vintage, she buys it, keeps it, and loves it with all her heart. And her heart is what I began to see with every spoken word! I began to see her heart peek through every facet of her, from the way she spoke to the way she lived, dressed, and loved. I realized that she genuinely loves everyone she talks to. It isn't that she *has* to talk to everyone; she just believes the best about everyone, finds magic in the everyday things around her, and *wants* to talk about it.

Becky was the friend I didn't know I needed. As weeks and months of friendship turned into years, it became clear that though we were opposites, our personalities meshed well. Like a tapestry of woven colors and threading, our differences made us beautiful together. I'm as opposite of her as one can get. I don't talk about my feelings unless I know the person extremely well, and I don't share my everyday business with everyone. I keep a tight inner circle of friends and only *they* know how I feel, why I feel it, who I care about, and what is important to me. I've never felt the need to wear my heart on my sleeve. But Becky does, and it's a beautiful thing to watch. She talks about her husband, her daughter, and her pets. She talks to everyone she can, everyone around her, and isn't afraid to speak her mind. This is who Becky is.

God orchestrates everything in our lives, and this was an orchestration that I never could have foreseen. I didn't know it when I met her, but a few years later, both of my best friends would move away from me—friends with whom I've had decades of time and relationship. Having Becky was a lifeline for me. God knew I would feel lost, but because of her, I wasn't alone—I had a kindred spirit alongside me. By saying yes to a friendship with her, by taking a leap of faith that she really could be good for me, my life is fuller than ever.

Becky's and my relationship has taught me to stop assuming things. For one, I don't assume life will stay the same. My two best friends moving away from me is proof of this. And second, I don't assume I know someone based on what I hear. Becky is a perfect example. Why should I assume to "know" a person because of the way they look? Why should I judge a person based on how they talk? I could've easily assumed so many things about Becky and never developed a relationship. What a loss that would've been!

Ten years later, we are still meeting up at thrift stores, still having coffee together, and still consider each other the greatest of friends. Her voice is still as gregarious and loud as ever… and I love it.

I'm honored God thought I could use someone like her in my inner circle, but it took faith on my part to pursue a friendship with a woman who is very different than me. It also took God's grace for me to look beyond first impressions and get over myself! Becky is a beautiful human with a style that is all her own. I'm honored to know her and hope to keep on thrifting and having coffee with her for as long as possible. Opposites attract, and I'm so grateful that they do.

The Tribe Makes It Better

Donna Collins Tinsley

I was around 40, with a baby on my hip and a toddler hanging onto my skirt, when I walked into the Winning Women Bible Study. My oldest daughter was 21 years older than my second child. When I went to the parks, libraries, and play places, most of the mothers were a lot younger than I was. I felt alone.

Motherhood the second time around, I must admit, was exhausting. I've been told that I looked like I had the cares of the world on my shoulders when I walked into Winning Women; even the long skirt and boots I wore that day looked heavy. But I was welcomed so sweetly.

My kids had never been to a nursery and were a bit wary, to say the least.

"Don't worry, honey," said a lady named Anita, who I soon learned was the teacher. "You don't have to put them in there. They can stay out here with you."

Her warm Southern drawl made me feel right at home; I'd been born in Chattanooga, Tennessee, myself. Beside her stood Nancy, a beautiful blonde, who gave me a hug and offered to find some toys for my girls to play with. She had some children around the age of mine, who were in the nursery.

Honestly, it was probably the hug I needed the most. That very first day, Nancy noticed the tears running down my cheeks while Anita taught.

She came right over after the teaching had ended. "Can I pray for you?"

I didn't even know if I could share what was in my heart. My oldest daughter had succumbed to a drug addiction that she'd picked up from her dad, my first husband, and the pain and despair ran deep.

> But Moses' hands got tired. So they got a stone and set it under him. He sat on it and Aaron and Hur held up his hands, one on each side.
>
> —EXODUS 17:12 (MSG)

"Please pray for my daughter, Regina," was all I could get out of my mouth, as the sobs started.

Nancy prayed a beautiful prayer. It filled me with peace, and after it was over I could even rest. After that, Anita always had Nancy check on me and all the women rallied around me, sitting by me so I didn't feel alone. I knew I'd found my tribe. It was pure sisterhood at its best.

Now I had something to look forward to each week. I kept going each Thursday. It gave me a reason to get out of the house and even dress up a bit. Eventually my girls also relaxed, and they started going into the nursery with the other kids.

Although the gathering was labeled a Bible study, to my heart it was pure worship. The most powerful part was the prayer time where we shared requests that were deep in our hearts. There were sisters there of all ages and backgrounds.

I had thought that I should wait until my life was "in order" to share my heart, but one day a woman came whose story changed my mind. She had cancer that was spreading rapidly.

"I just want to be able to live to see my youngest son graduate from high school." We all prayed hard for her. And even though in the end those prayers weren't answered in the way that we hoped, her story taught me that things don't have to be perfect in your life to ask for prayers. That day I vowed to share my story, even if it wasn't what I hoped or prayed for.

The truth was, although things had seemed to settle down some for Regina, her resolve to live a drug-free life had ended along with her marriage. After a painful divorce, she was no longer able to take care of her daughter, and the agony of that realization pushed her even further down the slippery slope of addiction. Her little girl came to live with us.

With the responsibility of taking care of her daughter gone, it was much easier for Regina to withdraw from family. Instead of getting treatment, her usage increased. She lost a very good job, her little house, and her self-respect.

In the nineties, it was hard to talk about the trauma a family goes through as they suffer along with their child who has succumbed to substance abuse. I didn't know if my new friends from Bible study would understand the pain we were going through or look down on our family. But each time I shared my heart and burdens, they joined together like Aaron and Hur holding up Moses's battle-weary arms.

Many were the prayers put on our prayer list, and pray they did.

"Please pray for Regina. I don't know where she is."

"Please pray for Regina. She is going to have a baby."

"Please pray for Regina. She is incarcerated."

And finally, years down the road, there were happier prayers:

"Pray for Regina, she is getting married."

"Pray for Regina—she and her husband are in treatment."

Through opening up about Regina's problems, I met Jane, who would soon become my best friend for life. She said the minute she saw me and heard me talk, she knew we would be friends.

"I knew when I heard your prayer requests that I could help you because I once battled drug use when I was young," she later told me.

Jane was about my age and, like me, had gotten pregnant late in life. Our group prayed when the doctor said the baby in her womb would have a genetic disorder. He was born as healthy as can be, with not a trace of the condition.

> And the peace of God, which transcends all understanding, will guard your hearts and your minds in Christ Jesus.
>
> —PHILIPPIANS 4:7 (NIV)

Once a year, Winning Women would have a retreat on St. Simon's Island, Georgia. I loved the peace and serenity there. To me there was no other place like it in the world. The first time I went, I was embraced by the lapping water and shady trees, and it felt like holy ground. The gentle water sounds comforted me as I walked to the little chapel by the river, which would become one of my favorite places. God's Spirit hovered over this place of love amid the beauty of nature. I felt like I was in another world, and I didn't want to leave.

Over the years the camaraderie I found there helped me to press on. The speakers gave me wisdom that I needed to become a better woman, wife, and mother. The first time I attended, the speaker had me laughing so hard that tears streamed down my face and I nearly fell off my chair. Other times, the weeping was real, for life can be hard even for a tribe of sisters who love one another. One year, the little baby I carried in my arms to that first meeting, Shiloh, went with me to play her guitar at early morning worship.

Now, many years down the road, many of the sisters I've written about have passed away, including Anita, the teacher who welcomed me and my daughters so sweetly.

I wish I could tell Anita, "Praise report! Regina and her husband are fifteen years in recovery. They just bought their first home. It is beautiful."

"Praise report! The granddaughter that we prayed for is doing great!"

"Praise report! Regina wants to come with me to retreat!"

The retreats are still going on, and there is a remnant of beautiful women who still love God and love one another. Last year, when Regina attended with me, the speaker had a story that Regina really related to, and she came away with a new outlook on life. My friends became her friends as we ate the sumptuous buffets, walked the beautiful grounds together, and made plans to go again. Every new day we find that we are better together.

Planting a Seed

Bettie Boswell

When I went to undergraduate school, I never imagined that
I would have a desire to become a teacher. Being a minister's
wife, I found myself instructing children on a weekly basis.
After a few years of teaching Sunday school classes, youth
groups, and leading songs for vacation Bible school, I grew to
love working with children and began to consider teaching as
a career.

My first step to grow my new future was to get a master's
degree that would certify me for an educator's license. One of
the requirements for certification included taking a biology
class, which did not thrill me in the least. Memories of taking high-school biology with a teacher who pushed disbelief
in God overwhelmed my thoughts. Then I heard that I could
get my master's degree through the Bible college I'd attended.
The school had recently made a cooperative agreement with a
university in order to offer a teaching degree. The exciting part
for me was that a Christian would be teaching the class that I'd
dreaded during my secondary education.

The instructor was a Christian named Betsy Dresser with
a brand-new doctorate degree. She started each of our classes
with short videos or slides displaying God's magnificent creation. Students were encouraged to take turns creating their
own visual presentations to share about the ways in which

God's beauty is found throughout the world. She used that tool to plant a seed in the heart of each student for the appreciation of creation.

Early in the semester she shared about the part of nature that fascinated her the most—the part that had inspired her to become a Christian: the microscopic organization of the animal and plant seeds used for reproduction. That aspect of biology had intrigued her and became her focus of study during her years of higher education.

Eventually, that interest led her to push the Cincinnati Zoo to create a frozen collection of embryos for saving endangered animals. Her research with those tiny parts of creation was groundbreaking at the time.

> I planted the seed, Apollos watered it, but God has been making it grow.
>
> —1 CORINTHIANS 3:6 (NIV)

The professor shared that when she noticed the uniqueness and organization of each cell, she began to wonder how something so complicated could come from the chaos that scientific knowledge had led her to believe was part of the beginnings of life. The way tiny nerves moved messages to our brains and made them perform intricate tasks was awe inspiring. How could these things work without the power of a creator? At that point in her studies she was not a Christian, but more and more she found that she couldn't understand how our biological processes could work without there being a master creator. Then she remembered a small spiritual seed planted during her childhood.

As a young girl, growing up between foster homes and her grandparent's care, she attended a vacation Bible school at a church near her home. Lessons presented during that single week mentioned God as the creator of all things. That dormant seed of knowledge grew from a memory to a desire to turn to the God who could make the complex and yet orderly natural world she loved to study.

My professor remembered the name of the church where she'd gone for those vacation Bible school lessons and went back to that same building, seeking the Lord. The teachers who had taught her years ago may not have been there to see the harvest of their teaching, but there were others at the church who led her to accepting Christ. Her budding faith showed her that the biology of natural life was a miraculous divine gift that science could demonstrate through careful examination.

Her work with the frozen zoo embryos brought worldwide attention to her efforts. Because of her persistence, many endangered species became part of her frozen embryo collection. Long after I knew her as a teacher, her early studies in this area would lead to DNA experiments and cloning. She became well-known in the Cincinnati area and within her new church home. From acquaintances in the congregation, she came in contact with someone who knew of the need for an adjunct biology professor to teach future Christian educators about God's approach to science. She blessed my college by stepping into the part-time instructor position.

Dr. Dresser's approach to science opened a door in my mind. I no longer dreaded it. When our class took a trip to the zoo, it was eye-opening. Going behind the scenes, encountering the animals up close and personal, and seeing some of her frozen embryos was an experience I would never forget. Science became interesting to me as I looked at the subject through God's eyes. As my courses continued, I went beyond the single

GOD'S GIFT OF TASTE
— Lynne Hartke —

DURING WORLD WAR II, George Washington Carver, a scientist and the director of the Agriculture Research and Experiment Station at the Tuskegee Institute, put out a pamphlet titled "Nature's Garden for Victory and Peace." The free manual had details on gathering and preparing edible wild plants and weeds to aid the war effort. The document included information for harvesting chicory, wild lettuce, pepper grass, wild garlic, and more than fifty other edible plants. At a time when many Americans were wondering how to feed their families, George Washington Carver reminded them that nature's garden—God and His creation—would meet all their needs.

---

biology class requirement and included several other science classes as electives.

My love of science grew so much that one of the professors from the cooperating college recommended that I teach science. I never found a science position, but I have included science in the general curriculum when I taught in elementary classrooms. As a music teacher, I had a fun unit on the science of sound and how instruments produce different tones. I've even used a few simple science experiments in Sunday school lessons to show the miracles of everyday life.

Being a firsthand witness to the miracle of God's creation transformed Betsy Dresser's life and caused the seed of her faith to flourish. In turn, she took my dread of science and turned it into a joy. I hope that I have planted a few seeds in children's hearts that will one day grow into a harvest for God's glory.

God Preserves the Faith We Share

A. J. Larry

Over the years, throughout the course of our Christian journey, my husband, John, and I have prayed earnestly for the preservation of our children, grandchildren, nieces, and nephews. But while we were able to witness God at work throughout their lives, there were other children we'd taught through years of Bible study, as far back as the 1980s, and we often wondered what had become of *them*.

Our questions had gone unanswered until we received a heartwarming surprise call from an esteemed minister friend of ours inviting us to visit their new church and school in Williston, Florida, about ninety minutes from our home. We accepted eagerly.

On the day of the planned visit, we left with what we assumed would be plenty of time. Our family of four had lived in Williston for a short time during the late eighties, and we knew that it was a small town, with only two traffic lights and almost everything in the town visible from the single main road through the area. *Who could get lost?*

But when we finally arrived, the church and school were nowhere to be seen. After several trips up and down that main road, with time ticking by and services due to begin soon, we finally gave in and called for directions. Pulling into the parking lot late and flustered, we were greeted by the pastor's daughter, whom we had last seen more than twenty years before, and slipped into the sanctuary.

Feeling awkward, we made our way along the side aisle and slipped quietly into the seats that suddenly appeared to be waiting for us. The joyful music quieted as our pastor-friend took his position on the pulpit to deliver the day's sermon.

When the message and altar call were delivered, the pastor caught sight of us. "Do you all remember him?" he asked casually, pointing at the tall young man with broad shoulders sitting at the opposite end of our pew.

We bent slightly, staring dubiously toward the other end of the row. "No," we had to admit.

> But Jesus said, "Leave the children alone, and do not forbid them to come to Me; for the kingdom of heaven belongs to such as these."
>
> —MATTHEW 19:14 (NASB)

The pastor continued, emphasizing that God's Word does not go out and return empty (Isaiah 55:11). He then introduced the man he'd pointed out—now age thirty-five—as the little boy who attended our in-home youth Bible study twenty-eight years prior. We were awestruck!

When we had first moved to Williston, our daughters had wholly disliked the small community until they'd met the little boy and his three sisters who lived next door. We also joined a local church. It was the church where we'd met our minister friend and his lovely family. Having glimpsed the bonding of our neighborhood kids, we had the idea to start a youth Bible study in our home, teaching children from ages ten to twelve on Thursday evenings. The Bible study quickly grew to ten eager young people. Our neighbors were the first to attend. Although the little boy next door was only seven years old, occasionally his two older sisters would allow him to tag along. Our prayer had been simple: that Scripture would carry those children for the rest of their lives.

> **So faith comes from hearing, that is, hearing the Good News about Christ.**
>
> —ROMANS 10:17 (NLT)

Now that we were made aware, hand in hand John and I humbly rose from our seats and slowly walked toward the opposite end of the pew. The broad-shouldered man met us halfway, and we embraced and cried together.

After the service, the now fully grown man told us that what he remembered most from our Bible study is how to talk to God. "It's what got me through my most difficult times in life." He told us about his family and gave a report on his sisters, the youngest of whom arrived at the end of the service after being informed that we were at the church. When she arrived, she sidled over and edged between us to share in the joyful reunion.

As the tears poured from my eyes, John and I marveled at the wonderful grace of God.

Hate is self-destructive. If you hate somebody, you're not hurting the person you hate. You're hurting yourself. . . . It's a real healing, forgiveness.

—Louis Zamperini, Olympic athlete

CHAPTER 4
Moving past Anger

Mr. Bobby
Bob Robertson, as told to Ginger Rue

"I am *not* doing it!" I seethed to my sister, Bea, on the phone. I tried to whisper so my wife, Jessica, wouldn't hear me from the other room.

"Come on, Bob," Bea said. "You can learn how to do anything."

"Not that!" I stopped short of demanding, *Haven't I done enough?* What more did God want from me?

It had all begun in November of 2007. We'd gone to visit my father-in-law a couple of hours from our home in Tuscaloosa, Alabama. He'd been diagnosed just a few days before with advanced lung and brain cancer. That Friday, when the last bell rang, Jessica told her students goodbye, and we rushed to her father's side. That night Jessica got up for a glass of water. I heard her calling my name from the kitchen.

"I can't move," she said, lying on the floor with her head against the cabinets. I called 911. They rushed her to the nearest emergency room, then helicoptered her to a trauma center in Chattanooga, Tennessee. One of the doctors used the word *quadriplegic*.

This couldn't be happening. Jess had simply reached up to get a glass, gotten dizzy, and fallen down. Healthy fifty-six-year-old women didn't just suddenly become quadriplegics from getting up to get a glass of water at night! Jess didn't deserve this. Everyone loved her—she was the sweetest, most giving person in the whole world. The only reason she was even in that kitchen, in that house, was that she was caring for her dad. Everything about this was just wrong.

Jess and I been married only eight years—years that had flown by because I'd never been so happy. In college we'd been fixed up by our friend Jamie, who'd insisted that we were perfect for each other. But for whatever reason, we'd just been friends. I married someone else and had three children, and Jessica stayed happily single, devoting herself to teaching and her church. It wasn't until many years later, after my divorce, that our paths had crossed again, and not by accident. Jamie invited Jessica to visit one weekend, then told her, "While you're here tonight, whether you like it or not, Bob Robertson is coming over." This time, I didn't let Jess get away. We dated two years and married in 1999.

> **Rejoice always, pray continually, give thanks in all circumstances; for this is God's will for you in Christ Jesus.**
>
> **—1 THESSALONIANS 5:16–18 (NIV)**

We'd led a quiet, cozy life together. Jessica loved cooking and doing needlework. She was an ideal stepmom to my children. Once our nest was empty, we focused on each other.

Just yesterday, we'd been safe at home, but now, Jess lay motionless in a trauma center.

Hours turned into days. "Bob, you haven't had a shower or changed clothes in over a week," Bea said. Had it been that long? A friend from church had called around Chattanooga, looking for a hotel where I could stay until Jess got better. I went there just long enough to shower and change. "No charge," the hotel clerk told me. "Your friend explained the situation. Stay as long as you need." I was so touched by the kindness. *This is just the sort of thing Jess would do for a stranger*, I thought. *God, please let her get well.*

Days turned into weeks, weeks into months. Jessica's father died while she was in the hospital, but she was too heavily medicated to understand. In January, they moved her to Birmingham—about an hour from home—but she still couldn't sit up. Just trying made her dizzy. We kept her room dark most of the time.

Sometimes, when she was lucid, Jessica would tell me what she'd been praying for. "Bob, I asked God if every fifteen minutes, He would let something good happen to remind us He's with us." That was so Jess. Instead of focusing on what had been taken from her, she looked for joy, finding it in a cheerful nurse or a friend's card or phone call. Jess was so loving and good; how could God let this happen to her? But I wouldn't allow myself to get angry. I owed it to Jess not to get upset.

By the end of March, the doctors in Birmingham decided Jess could come home because she was able to sit up for thirty minutes. Back at home and finally alone for the first time in months, Jessica said we needed to talk.

"This isn't fair to you, Bob," she said. "I may never walk again. I may never get my arms and hands back. I want you to divorce me and put me in a nursing home. I want you to live your life."

I laughed. I couldn't help it. It was the most ridiculous thing I'd ever heard.

"I'm serious," Jess said. "I want you to live your life."

"I am living my life," I said. "You are my life."

I made her promise never to suggest it again.

Gradually, we settled into a routine. My company been kind enough to hold my job until I could get back. We hired a caregiver during the week, and on Saturdays, "Jessica's Dream Team," as we called her friends from church, would take turns helping to work her muscles and joints. Eventually, Jess was able to move her arms again. That gave us hope, even though she'd shown no signs of improvement in her trunk or legs.

"You know what, Bob? I've decided walking is overrated," Jess said one day. "If I could choose, I'd rather have my hands so I could do my needlework again. Hands are a miracle." My wife, who before the accident had walked five miles a day, had

> **Do not be anxious about anything, but in every situation, by prayer and petition, with thanksgiving, present your requests to God.**
>
> **—PHILIPPIANS 4:6 (NIV)**

such a small request—surely God would oblige. *Lord, look how much progress she's made in six months!* I prayed. *Please, God, let her get back to normal.*

It took almost my whole paycheck to afford Jessica's caregiver, so we decided I'd retire early. With more time together, we watched movies, talked, read the Bible. We studied the book of Job. I wanted to have that kind of faith, like Jess did. I like to think I did a pretty good job...most of the time.

Sometimes, though, I'd have a hard time keeping it together. Like the time when I'd driven her to church and a rainstorm came on our drive home. Her wheelchair had slipped off the ramp, and when I'd tried to catch it, Jess and I had both wound up sprawled on the wet grass as buckets of water poured from the sky. My shin gushed blood from hitting the ramp when I'd tried to grab the wheelchair before Jess fell. I'd never been so angry in my life. Didn't God recognize that I was taking my paralyzed wife to church? How could He not only fail to reward that, but instead, seemingly, to punish us for it? Times like that, it just seemed like maybe God wasn't holding up His end of the deal. *Come on, Lord!* I demanded from time to time. *Help a guy out!*

And that's exactly how I was feeling on the phone that day with Bea.

With my early retirement and Jess's medical bills, money was tight. Having Jess's hair washed and rolled twice a week at the beauty parlor was too expensive. Jessica's hairstylist volunteered to give me a hands-on tutorial: wash Jessica's hair, apply two thickening products plus a curling gel, roll sections of hair backward in Velcro rollers, pin, and blow dry. And that was the easy part! I was also supposed to somehow part Jessica's hair in a certain type of zigzag instead of a straight line so that the curls would fall correctly. A purposely crooked part? Three styling products? All those little pink rollers? How did women stand it all? It was ridiculous!

Which was why I was telling Bea how I adamantly refused to do it.

"I shouldn't have to roll hair!" I complained. "I don't even *have* any hair!"

"You can do it," Bea insisted again.

"But...I don't want to!"

And wasn't that what it was really all about? I didn't want it. Any of it.

I didn't want Jessica to be in a wheelchair…to not be able to do her needlework…to feel like a burden. I didn't want any of the changes that had come with this horrible accident. I didn't want the accident to have ever even happened. I wanted to go back in time, to wish it away, to change the terrible twist of fate that had robbed my wonderful wife of the life she deserved. I just wanted things to go back to normal. Why couldn't God understand that?

"OK, Bob," said Bea. "Fine. Don't roll Jessica's hair. Take her to the beauty parlor twice a week."

After I hung up the phone with Bea, I was still frustrated—maybe even more so. I had a lot of praying to do.

I thought about Jesus telling the paralyzed man He healed at the pool on the Sabbath to pick up his bed

For we live by faith, not by sight.

—2 CORINTHIANS 5:7 (NIV)

and walk. Of His telling the blind man to go and wash in the pool of Siloam. Why would the paralyzed man want to even touch the bed he'd been lying on for thirty-eight years? Why did the blind man have to wash his eyes when Jesus could have easily just spoken the words to miraculously heal him? But neither of these men asked questions. Instead, they both stepped out in faith. And even though I didn't understand why I had to style hair on top of everything else, I had to step out in faith, too, and believe that God would work with me as I helped Jessica.

It was never really about the hair. It was about giving thanks in all circumstances, about walking by faith and not by sight. It was about trusting God. Since Jess's accident, I have had to do so many things I never even thought about doing, and God has been with me every step of the way.

Jess and I still often laugh about the fact that a reluctant bald man is now her hairdresser. We've even made a game of the whole thing. We set the DVR to record *Jeopardy!* every day, and I try to beat my best time or at least finish her hair before the Daily Double. I never do, but we get a kick out of trying. I've even perfected the notorious zigzag part, and when Jess's friends tell her how pretty she looks, she says, "Have you met my hair-dresser, Mr. Bobby? He's highly exclusive, but he's the best!"

And you know what? She's right. I am, actually, a pretty great hairdresser.

Who's Your Daddy?

Donna Collins Tinsley

"Donna, get in the car. I'll take you home from school."

I was about seven years old, on my way down the little country road that ran from the Chattanooga Valley school to the street where I lived. My grandmother, who I simply called Nanny, would be waiting for me with a cup of hot chocolate or some other snack. It didn't take long to walk there, maybe about 15 minutes. As I peered into the car, I recognized the man talking as my dad. But I shook my head no.

"What's wrong, honey?" he said in his slow Southern drawl.

Sensitive as I was, I didn't want to hurt his feelings. I didn't want to tell him that he was a stranger to me, and I wasn't allowed to get in the car with strangers. He was in the military, and he and my mother had never lived together, as far as I knew; I knew his face through pictures and through occasional visits when he was on leave, but he was a stranger to me.

Sad to say, he remained that—a stranger who was a dad only in name.

At Nanny's house there was love, food, and church every time the doors of the church were opened. She was the church pianist and also the local music teacher. She taught music lessons for fifty cents an hour or would barter with people if they couldn't afford her fees. It was at that church, Flintstone

Baptist Church in Chattanooga Valley, that I went forward as a child to accept God into my life.

It was an otherwise ordinary Sunday when I was touched by the altar call and started getting out of my seat, heading to the front of the church.

As I got up, I felt Nanny tugging on my dress. "Wait till your mom is here to see you, honey!" she whispered.

I don't know why the urgency within me was so strong, but I pulled away. "No, Nanny, I must go now." Much later, I would realize that it was my hunger for a father that drew me to the altar as a young girl. Because for those of us who've lived life without an earthly father's love, there will always be a real father—Jesus.

Not long after, I went from the music and serenity of my Nanny's house to the violence and chaos of my stepfather's home in Florida. Mama had remarried, had three more children, and wanted me to join them. I didn't want to leave the only home I'd ever known, but as a child, I had no choice. A couple of years later, my stepfather was sent to prison for abusing me. Mama was all alone raising four children on her own.

I lost contact with my biological father, the one who wanted to give me a ride home.

Like many girls raised without a good father figure, I sought love at a young age. By the time I was fifteen, I was married and pregnant. My mom remarried, but I never felt close to my new stepfather because I really didn't trust men. *Dads,* I thought. *Who needs them?* I could count on the fingers of one hand the men I trusted and still have some fingers left over. That's a sad statement, and I say it to my shame, but it really was my reality. And then the day came that I realized I'd married someone just like my stepfather. My heart was not only broken but hardened once again to the need for a father.

Some years later, I remarried, and I did find a good dad for my daughter. Although I'd pretended all my life that I really didn't care if I had an earthly father, sometimes I'd hear people talking about their dads and what a precious relationship they have or have had, and I felt a soul-wrenching father-hunger. I never had that experience of being father's little princess and feeling cherished. I've been brought to tears hearing someone's memories of lying upon their father's chest as a child and feeling his scratchy beard.

> There you saw how the LORD your God carried you, as a father carries his son, all the way you went until you reached this place.
>
> —DEUTERONOMY 1:31 (NIV)

Life went on, and eventually my curiosity about my family history led me to connect with some of my biological dad's family, although he had passed away by that point. I even took some DNA tests, and they revealed a well-kept secret: the man I thought was my father was not. I was shocked and saddened to once again lose my father, and to discover my real biological father was someone I would never know.

Around this time, I was impressed in my heart that God was going to heal me of my father-hunger on Father's Day in 2023. In anticipation of this, I signed up to bless the communion that day at church, as we are allowed to share what is on our heart a bit when blessing the elements.

The big day arrived. When I walked up to the pulpit, I said, "Happy Father's Day. I am so happy for those of you who had a perfect father, the one of their dreams. Sadly, not everyone has had that experience. But I want to share something that happened to me recently."

I shared with them that I'd recently seen a Facebook game where if you touch the image of a chair, you will see who is always with you. I don't often do those, but I was compelled to try this one.

When I tapped the chair, the answer came up: *your Father.* Well, at first I dismissed that, since I now knew that I'd probably never met my biological father.

But immediately in my heart, the Lord reminded me that He, my heavenly Father, was exactly what was said on the chair test: *He was always by my side, and He always watched over me!* I took the same test later, thinking it probably would give different results, but the same word came: *father.* I realized that it was God trying to get a word of love to me.

"It's been hard to understand why I never got to meet my own father," I continued. "Part of me acknowledges that it was that father-hunger that drew me to Jesus. My need was greater at a much younger age than many other people's need, I feel.

"I have a much deeper relationship with the Lord than I might have had if I'd grown up with a good earthly father. I ran to the Lord early and clung to Him through much heartache and pain as a child.

"I know and believe that He was always watching, sometimes weeping, at the things I went through when younger, but He never turned away and always gave me a word to hang on to. One of the best gifts in the world to me is the Word of God.

GOD'S GIFT OF TOUCH
— Lynne Hartke —

HAVE YOU HEARD of "skin hunger"? It's a term used to describe our longing to be touched. We don't need to interact with others to experience the softness of a rose petal, the roughness of sandpaper, the coolness of an ice cube, or the warmth of an electric blanket. But our skin reminds us that we were created to be touched. From newborn babies to octogenarians, people's stress levels lower and their sense of well-being increases when others hug and touch them, making them feel calmer and happier. In a world that increasingly separates people with virtual screens, it is important to remember to reach out and touch others. Our skin needs it.

"So, yes, I'll accept that my Father was not only sitting next to me, but holding me, escorting me, and rejoicing over me, my whole life through. I don't have to wonder why the circumstances of my birth were the way they were. I don't have to wonder why I have the DNA that I have. I'll take the DNA of the Lord my God, and heavenly Father any day. He is a good, good father. The best!

"I wanted to serve communion today because the Lord told me He was going to heal me this very day, at age seventy-two, of all those hurts, pains, and broken dreams of being a girl not knowing her father. He is the ultimate Father, the love of my life, my everything. Let us commune with Him as we take of his body and his blood today in remembrance of him."

I went to my seat, wondering if I'd done the right thing by sharing some painful things with a whole congregation. Afterward, though, a lady in her nineties came over to me and revealed that she'd never felt her own father's love. Several men said they related to my story also.

Today we know that although many of us did not have that true "father" experience while here on earth, our time in eternity together with the one true Father, the One who never disappoints, will be a dream come true. God as my father has been a constant presence in my life, as a young girl and now even to my old age. I pray that there will be healing for any of us who have experienced the pain of father-hunger.

Betrayed but Not Broken

Lisa Toney

Ten years of laughter. Ten years of memories. Ten years of friendship. When you find a kindred spirit, it is a gift straight from heaven. Best friends enjoy a deep connection and shared perspective on life. In the mirror of friendship, we discover our support system. A friendship that endures through the years builds trust that gives you confidence because it helps you navigate the ups and downs of life. Friends stand by your side through the good, the bad, and the ugly. Friendships are so special—so rare— and they are supposed to withstand any challenge.

Until they don't. I'm still not sure what went wrong.

I had a good thing going. I had been dating a fantastic guy who was smart, funny, and kind. We had been dating for two-and-a-half years, and I was madly in love; I thought I'd marry him someday. It was a beautiful time in my life. I had an amazing best friend and a boyfriend I was crazy about. In fact, the three of us would sometimes hang out and spend time together…

You know where this is going, right?

I didn't. It completely caught me off guard. One day I noticed she laughed a little longer at his jokes. She touched his shoulder when she talked to him. I was jolted by the reality deep in my bones: something was terribly wrong. Something had changed. I soon discovered they had been seeing each other behind my back, and he wanted to be with her instead of me. Knife to the heart and stabbed in the back at the same time. Betrayal. Double betrayal.

I was crushed. Devastated. My whole world imploded. I couldn't get my head around what was happening. I was livid at him. I thought he loved me. I thought he cared. I thought we were on the same page. But as angry as I was at him, I found myself even more enraged by my best friend's betrayal. Best friends are not supposed to do that to each other. The two people I turned to for emotional support were suddenly ripped out of my life. The two people I trusted and dearly loved disconnected themselves from me. I was left in the dust and was emotionally bleeding out.

> **Be kind to one another, tenderhearted, forgiving one another, as God in Christ forgave you.**
>
> —EPHESIANS 4:32 (ESV)

I became haunted by questions. *How could two people I had spent so much time with and knew so well do this? What did I do wrong? Why don't they care about me anymore? What is wrong with me? Why would God let this happen to me? Is God mad at me?* It became freakishly hard to trust my ability to make decisions. I thought I had made a good decision to trust and depend on these two people. Praying became hard to do. Hurt seemed to fill every moment and space in my head and heart.

I found myself living with rage like I had never known. I was so angry. So. So. Angry. I had never known anger like that before. It was intense, stifling, consuming… and awful. Sleeping and eating became difficult. The darkness of depression swirled around me. I no longer trusted anyone or liked the person I saw in the mirror in the morning.

As a follower of Jesus, I knew I *should* forgive, but I didn't know how. I didn't want to say words of forgiveness that I didn't really mean and did not feel. I was stuck.

My mentor met with me one day, sat beside me, and gently asked what happened. Through tears, I shared my broken heart. My life was broken. I was broken.

He disagreed! *What?* He looked me in the eye and reminded me that I followed Jesus, which made all the difference when we were at the end of ourselves. Jesus binds up broken hearts. Jesus is strong when we are weak. Jesus helps us to forgive our past so we can shape our future. I gulped, knowing he was right and wanting to get free from the ugliness that I was living in every day. Hate, rage, and anger were lousy friends. I didn't like who I was, and I was scared about who they would shape me to become.

So every night, as my head hit the pillow, I breathed out a prayer for something I knew only Jesus could do: "Help me to forgive them." Night after night after night. The same process. The same words.

I'm unsure if that is the same approach I'd take now, but that was all I could do. God knew how defeated I felt. Those few words were all I could get out of my shattered spirit.

As I look back, I think that every night God used that prayer to take one of those deeply embedded ragged shards and remove it. I didn't know it at the time. I didn't *feel* it. At times I wondered if my prayers mattered. I wondered if God really would help me. I wondered if I could get free from my pain.

As I was going through this process, I discovered that Jesus said something radical about forgiveness: "But if you do not forgive others their sins, your Father will not forgive your sins" (Matthew 6:15, NIV).

Forgiveness was absolutely essential as a follower of Jesus. I persisted with my meager prayer, unsure what to expect or how to file down those sharp edges of pain piercing my life.

> **And whenever you stand praying, forgive, if you have anything against anyone, so that your Father who also is in heaven may forgive you your trespasses.**
>
> —MARK 11:25 (ESV)

As I went on, I pondered if Jesus was really enough for me. If people could mistreat one another and cause so much pain, could the ways of Jesus really impact this world and make a difference?

God led me to two verses I held on to with my whole being. I'm italicizing the words that hit me the hardest here: "This day I call the heavens and the earth as witnesses against you that I have set before you life and death, blessings and curses. Now choose life, so that you and your children may live and that you may *love* the LORD your God, *listen* to his voice, and *hold* fast to him. *For the LORD is your life*" (Deuteronomy 30:19–20, NIV).

Day after day, I prayed my prayer for forgiveness. Days turned into weeks. Weeks turned into months. For four months I prayed that prayer. I held on to Jesus. I focused my head and heart.

Love the Lord. Listen for His voice. Hold fast to Jesus. The Lord is my life.

I came to believe He is enough.

One day it happened. I don't know why. There was nothing special about that day. I ran into my former best friend in a parking lot. I realized all the hate, pain, and rage were no longer there. In the midst of a conversation that lasted a few brief sentences, I said the words I never thought I'd say: "I forgive you."

Although forgiven, our friendship was not restored. There was just too much hurt to reestablish trust. But I was able to move forward and create a better future for myself. I had been betrayed, but because of Jesus, I was not broken. God can transform our pain into strength we didn't know was there. Recovery is the art of reassembly. It takes hard work. It takes time. It takes Jesus.

Shattered dreams can become new beginnings. Shattered hearts can carve out newfound compassion for others. And shattered souls can encounter a God who puts hearts and lives back together.

Scars are the proof that healing is possible.

Anger, Dementia, God

Margaret Best

Every night I prayed: "Lord, take this awful dementia from my father. He's a good man. He's lived a God-filled life. Why does he have to suffer such confusion?" I attended church, opened the Bible, and tried to read, but nothing made sense. I walked in a fog. There seemed to be a fence I couldn't climb preventing me from receiving God's grace.

For many years I had noticed a constant decline in my father's mental capacities. Slowly, he lost the ability to make decisions and follow written instructions. He misplaced items and repeated questions already answered. His once-sparkling hazel eyes dimmed as he struggled to understand simple directions or conversations. Frequently he wandered lost in a familiar neighborhood.

Mother refused to believe Dad had dementia. He continued to drive, which scared me, but Mother insisted he drove better than she. "All he needs is for someone to tell him where to go and when to turn. He's just getting old."

Wanting to help in any way possible, my husband and I often drove to my parents' home six hours away. Still, Mother refused any help we offered.

Then Dad suffered a major stroke. As a result, the doctor placed my father in the veteran's home close by. Mother often called requesting our assistance. We arrived, escorted Mother to the home, and then sat with her as she argued with the doctors and Dad's caregivers.

Every night I prayed: "Lord, if you are not going to take the dementia from my father, at least send your spirit of wisdom to Mother so she will make the proper decisions." But Mother stubbornly refused to accept the reality that my father had dementia and needed special-ized care and medication, and she repeatedly refused to give doctors permission to treat him. Nothing we said and did could change her mind.

If my father's illness and mother's obstinacy had been the only difficulties, perhaps I could have handled my life better, but we were supporting our son while his marriage died, selling our home of twenty years, and packing for

> **My God, my God, why have you forsaken me? Why are you so far from saving me, so far from my cries of anguish?**
>
> **—PSALM 22:1 (NIV)**

a move out of the country. Anger took root. I became mad at my mother, my husband, and myself. I walked in a dark space, feeling helpless and overwhelmed. Neither the Bible, prayer, nor church made sense. I felt as lost as my father must have been. This continued until a few weeks before we were to leave for our next missionary assignment.

My friend called. "My church is sponsoring a Christian three-day weekend called *Via de Cristo.* I have an invitation for you. Would you like to come?"

I had been angry for so long. It became a way of life. Knowing God had not caused these problems, my displaced anger turned on my husband and myself. I lived in a black cave surrounded by dark, growling wolves feeding my irritations. Perhaps this would be a way out.

"I'll pick you up this afternoon," my friend offered. She knew I had wanted to go to one of these retreats for a long time, but she also knew some of the many personal challenges I was facing. "If you don't want to stay, I'll take you home."

> A person's own folly leads to their ruin, yet their heart rages against the LORD.
>
> —PROVERBS 19:3 (NIV)

She and I joined many other women from differing denominations for the *Via de Cristo* weekend. During the weekend, we slept together on cots with our own pillows. We laughed, cried, played, ate, and studied together. While attending workshops about creating better lives through Jesus Christ, we shared intimate problems.

Six women, including me, formed a circle in a small side room for group prayer. These strangers and I prayed in solemn voices, until I raised my eyes to the sky and blurted out: "I'm mad. I'm angry at you, God!"

Silence and shock filled the room. I continued yelling at God. "I cannot be angry at you. You are omnipotent, the King of Kings, the Almighty, but I am mad! Why have you allowed my father to linger in this limbo for so long?" My rant continued uninterrupted for at least ten minutes, anger building and flowing out of me. We held one another close, shaking and crying. I became weak, my knees buckled, and we sat on the sofa chairs until our crying stopped and we began to sing.

A heavy load was lifted from my shoulders that day, transported into space, and burned up in the sun. God healed me of my anger that day, and when I returned home, that healing allowed me to continue making decisions and plans without worry for my parents.

No miracle occurred. My Dad's dementia continued for three more years. My son got a divorce but continued seeing his children; my brother moved next door to my mother to help her while I was gone. The house sold and the move was completed without disturbance. I joined a new church, became active in it,

> **In this world you will have trouble. But take heart! I have overcome the world.**
>
> —JOHN 16:33 (NIV)

read the Bible, and held meetings in my new home. Best of all, my father waited until we returned from our assignment, and my children and their children had a chance to visit him before he passed away.

That healing experience saved my Christian life, helping me deal with anger, dementia, and God. I learned God is all-powerful, loving, large enough to carry the weight of the world and all our rage. This deep experience of the ways that God forgives taught me that He is so powerful, so loving, that He can allow His people to become angry at Him, forgive them, and bring them peace.

Walk of Faith

Raymond Duval

There are moments in my life that were defining. Holding my newborn child in my arms and promising to watch over her throughout life. Praying over my child as I held her in my arms as an adult, watching as she became a fragile mess due to a life-threatening disease. Watching helplessly as she fought for life. I saw her first steps, and now, as I looked at her confined to a wheelchair, I found myself wondering if she would ever walk again, let alone claim victory over the disease that had waged all-out war on her body.

As a parent, I had taught my daughter, Bridgette, how to be a good Christian, and I celebrated as she embraced God and His teachings. During the good times in life, I saw her joy and undying love for her heavenly Father. When illness set in, her faith was challenged. She began to question God's love as she battled each day to survive.

The elusive question "Why?" was forefront in her mind, and with no concrete answer available, anger began to consume her. Would that be the portal that allowed evil to enter her thoughts in hopes of reconfiguring them to a non-Christian belief system? Was this where I as a parent would start to question my own faith and beliefs? How strong was my faith, and was it enough for both of us?

Why her? What has she done to deserve this? How can a heavenly Father who is all loving hurt those that He supposedly loves? How can I, her earthly father, continue to tell her that God will heal her as we both watch a once successful and vibrant woman fade away?

With a diagnosis of "critical and manageable until your death" bestowed upon my child, I was forced to face the reality that Bridgette might not win the fight against the disease. I tried understanding the diagnosis, but I couldn't get past the reality of the situation. I broke down in tears as I prayed, "Dear Lord, please give me my child's pain. She's so young, and I have been gifted a wonderful life to this point. Let her be pain-free, and let her live her life to the fullest." As I waited in silence for an answer, I tried to bargain with God. *If I do this, will you please do that?*

> ## And whatever you ask in prayer, you will receive, if you have faith.
>
> —MATTHEW 21:22 (ESV)

The disease reached a point where Bridgette was confined to a wheelchair. She had no strength to even sit up in that chair, and she even lost her sight, hearing, and speech for a period. I once again told her that God would heal her. This time, her response delivered the most pain that I have ever felt in my life. She spoke three words that brutally carved through my heart and soul like a sharp knife.

"I hate God."

I hate God. What does that even mean? The pain associated with that phrase is hard to hear from anyone, anywhere. Hearing it from Bridgette felt like my heart and soul were ripped wide open, vandalized, and left bleeding and abused. Tears of pain, confusion, and fear started to flow from my eyes.

In the days and nights after her declaration of hate, I prayed continuously to God. This time, though, I asked for strength, guidance, and direction. I determined that the only way I was going to be able to walk Bridgette back to the Lord was if my faith was so strong that it would act as a guiding light for her.

★★★

My daughter had a horse that she loved dearly, Fearless Warrior. To her, he represented life. Since the onset of the disease, her horse had become her will to fight for life.

> **But Jesus on hearing this answered him, "Do not fear; only believe, and she will be well."**
>
> —LUKE 8:50 (ESV)

One night we entered the silent barn to visit her horse. As I wheeled her into the barn, Fearless Warrior was calling out to her. When we came close to his stall, he put his head in her lap as she sat unmoving in her wheelchair. Mustering all her strength, she reached out and ran her fingers through his mane for a few minutes. Later she would tell me that to her it seemed like hours. As their eyes met, I sensed that the horse was giving her a message and trying to transfer his strength to her through the deep bond that they had built throughout the years.

I thought, *Could this be God using her horse to heal her?*

Many conversations between Bridgette and me ensued, some productive and others more like volleys in a war. So many times, I would find a quiet place to cry, pray, and rejuvenate my faith. Each prayer was for continued strength and guidance. Each prayer was focused on my ability to be strong enough to overcome her present lack of faith.

It was not until Bridgette asked to see her horse again that her world started to change. This time, she asked us to let her sit on Fearless Warrior. We hoisted her from her wheelchair and put her on his back. I prayed silently to God, asking that He intercede and use her horse to help heal her. Then I saw the tears flow from my daughter's eyes. They were not the tears of hate and anger I'd seen so often recently. Her face and body radiated of redemption, love, and new purpose.

> Now therefore go, and I will be with your mouth and teach you what you shall speak.
>
> —EXODUS 4:12 (ESV)

As we lifted her off her horse and attempted to put her back in her wheelchair, she instead wrapped her arms around Fearless Warrior's neck and stood where she was for a moment. As they both gazed into each other's eyes, she started to take her second set of first steps. Slowly—the clock on the wall said it took over an hour—they walked toward his stall, twenty feet away.

God gifted us a miracle that night, one that has never stopped reverberating through our lives. Bridgette's first steps that night were a foreshadowing of the journey that she would take as she started her walk back to her heavenly Father. As her faith became stronger, her ability to trust in the Lord became

GOD'S GIFT OF TOUCH
— Heidi Gaul —

But while he was still a long way off, his father saw him and was filled with compassion for him; he ran to his son, threw his arms around him and kissed him. —Luke 15:20 (NIV)

MANY OF US lived in rebellion against faith and authority growing up. I know I did. But when my child followed in my footsteps, I learned it's possible to hunger for the touch of a loved one. When at last she returned, I felt the hug we exchanged throughout my entire body. My—our—healing began in those precious moments.

---

stronger as well. Her pain was replaced with a calm and peace that is something to behold.

The medical community told her to not run or exercise. This would be certain death, they said. Bridgette said, "I trust in the Lord," and together she and God rewired her body so that it needed exercise to exist.

A year and a half after her second set of first steps, she ran a full marathon, something that the doctors had said she would never do. God said, "Take My hand, and we will run it together."

God allowed me, through prayer, to strengthen my faith. He allowed me to be a beacon that would show my daughter the way back to His eternal light. Through the gift of a miracle that He gave to Bridgette, the use of her horse, and the strength and guidance He gave to me, my daughter has been saved.

Call it a clan, call it a network, call it a tribe, call it a family: Whatever you call it, whoever you are, you need one.

—Jane Howard, journalist

CHAPTER 5

Lifted by Family

Who Would Have Thought?

Elsa Kok Colopy

It was not a good day. Sitting outside the service garage, I buried my face in my hands. Seriously? How could I need four new tires? I knew the mechanic was right, especially when he showed me the balding area on two of the tires. My car was a death trap. Or so his raised eyebrows and shaking head seemed to say.

My hope had been far different from this reality. I was expected at a family reunion in Colorado in one week. As a single mom, I felt oh-so-responsible and wise going to the mechanic so he could give my car the once-over before the 700-mile trip. He was supposed to say that I would do great, the car would do better, and those 700 miles would fly by on the wings of cruise control. I had saved just enough money to be able to afford the gas and the food. Tires were not in the budget.

Shame covered me like an itchy wool sweater. I was the youngest child of five. All of my brothers (and their adorable families) were in a good place financially—and in life. I was the only one divorced, the only one scraping by, the only one making two bad decisions for every good one. I knew Jesus. Well, I knew of His grace. I'd leaned heavily into His mercy a million times over the years prior, and my heart was tender to His kindness. I'd come to depend on Him for nearly everything, trying not to feel like a nuisance as I called on Him every single day.

Oh, Jesus, I prayed. *Here I am again. I'm trying so hard and it just feels like I can't get a break. Please, Lord, will You help me? Miraculously fix my tires? Provide for new ones? Any other creative solution would be good, because I'm fresh out of hope.*

It didn't even occur to me to ask my family for help. They were kind people, for sure, but we'd been raised to be independent. My dad was an inventor and engineer who had immigrated to the United States from the Netherlands. He was stoic and hardworking, and approached parenting with a dry and logical mindset. If we wanted something, we were to work hard to get it. I was an adult now, with a little girl of my own. I was supposed to provide for her on my own, and that was that.

And my God will meet all your needs according to the riches of his glory in Christ Jesus.

—PHILIPPIANS 4:19 (NIV)

The next few days dragged by as I looked toward my departure date. I shared with a few friends what I was going through and asked them to pray. Two days before my trip I got a call from one of those friends. "Elsa, I can get you to the reunion! My husband is traveling and we have a spare car for the week. You can use ours!"

Tears sprang to my eyes. "Really? Are you sure?" She was. *Oh, God, thank You,* I whispered. *Thank You so much!* I didn't think about where I would get the money to fix the bald tires on my own car. If God had a solution for the reunion trip, I was certain He had a plan for the tires. I could trust Him.

My daughter Samantha and I packed up just a few days later and hit the road. We worshipped in the car, be-bopping our way down the highway. We chair-danced through Kansas and doo-wopped through the eastern part of Colorado. Late that evening, we pulled up to the rented house and ran into the welcoming arms of my brothers, mom, and dad. Samantha scampered off with her cousins to catch up on all things of preteen importance. I thanked God for my benefactor and for a safe arrival to my family.

The days flew by quickly as we explored the mountains and caught up with one another and our lives. Halfway through the week, the men took off for their traditional reunion catch-up time. When the women went on these ventures, it was usually an all-day affair—we'd start with breakfast, break for shopping, and then dive into lunch. The guys usually ate breakfast together, shared a few words, and called it good. After the men left, the women and the kids took off to town to shop for souvenirs and see what kind of free fun we could find. It was nearly two when we returned and the guys still weren't back. Unusual, but we took full advantage by heading back out and seeing what other trouble we could get into.

It was nearly four o'clock when we arrived back at the mountain rental. Immediately we noticed something strange—all the men were now standing outside in the driveway. Uh-oh. Apparently we'd pushed our luck just a little too far and were back too late. My girl and I climbed out of the back seat, ready to share the very good reason we'd been gone so long. I walked toward my dad and then noticed he had a silly smile on his face. As a stoic Dutch man, he was not given to silly smiles, so I wondered what was up.

He held out his hand, a set of keys dangling from his fingertips.

I looked at him. I looked at the keys. I glanced to my left to see my four brothers standing with the same goofy grins. They moved apart, and behind them sat a small red car. On the windshield was a large red bow. My brain tried to take it in. I looked from my dad to my brothers to the beautiful sporty car in the driveway. And back again. Dad had tears in his eyes.

"Is that—" I was almost afraid to ask. "Is that mine?"

He nodded.

I burst into tears and wrapped my arms around his neck. Samantha chirped beside me. "It's ours, Mommy? Is it ours? Does it have a clock?"

I laughed. Clocks were very important to my girl. She liked to know the time, the plan, the exact next step in every situation.

"Shall we find out?"

> **If you, then, though you are evil, know how to give good gifts to your children, how much more will your Father in heaven give good gifts to those who ask him!**
>
> **—MATTHEW 7:11 (NIV)**

We took the keys and ran over to the car. I ran my hand along the cool red exterior, my tears smudging the sleek lines in my vision. I opened the door and climbed in, while Samantha jumped into the passenger seat. We turned the key. I pointed to the small display where the time shone brightly. "It has a clock, baby."

"Oh yay!"

Later that evening I leaned against my dad's shoulder. "That was the last thing on earth I would have expected."

He smiled. "Good. I had to check with your brothers because I never did anything like that for them. But they've all seen how hard you've been working. I've seen how hard you've been working. They were excited and went with me to the dealership today, helped me negotiate the details, and here we are. I love you."

Tears again. "I love you, too, Dad."

I raised my eyes to heaven and whispered to my God, "Now You're just showing off…"

A Megaphone for God's Grace

Laurie Davies

My mother-in-law, Lucy, looked helplessly at her fork. Once the undisputed matriarch of her large Italian brood, she no longer presided over the chaos and conversation of our family get-togethers. Chatter in the next room drowned out the low hum and clicks of her oxygen tank.

She glanced at the tender roast beef, then sighed heavily and turned her head.

Is she just not hungry? Does she need help remembering how to hold the fork? Will I insult her if I help?

I risked it. I slid over to the chair next to hers, sliced a small piece of roast, and held it to her lips. She focused on me intently before gratefully accepting the bite of food.

"I know I should know who you are," she said. "Thank you for being kind to me."

She glanced back down at her plate, her eyes asking for another bite. Her brushed silver hair was soft on this Sunday. So was her demeanor. It wasn't always that way.

"I'm Laurie. I'm married to your youngest son, Greg," I said, scooping a toddler-sized bite of mashed potatoes to her lips. I bit my tongue hard, so that my voice would not break. "You're the reason I know Jesus."

"Really?" she said, her smile as big as her Italian personality. "Jesus." She slipped into whatever sweet moment of memory her declining mind could summon.

I looked out the front picture window. I wondered if I would even know God if not for the restless, relentless faith pursuit of the woman whose fork I now held. She spent half of her adult life working a puzzle that had a missing piece.

The piece was grace.

And it entirely transformed her life. Then her son's. Then mine.

★★★

Lucy's survival story is the stuff of legend among my in-laws. Born premature into a very poor coal-mining region in 1927, Lucy Cocca's tiny infant body was wrapped in cotton and placed into a drawer near the fireplace. Her relatives kept watch on her to keep her warm and alive.

> **And as God's grace reaches more and more people, there will be great thanksgiving, and God will receive more and more glory.**
>
> —2 CORINTHIANS 4:15 (NLT)

She was born a fighter. But, as she would later admit, all her fight and spiritedness had its dark side too. "Mama Lucia" was restless and fiery, sometimes aiming that fire at her family. On balance, she was her five kids' number-one fan, never missing a game, a swim meet, or the chance to take the baby—my husband—to eat hamburgers at the mall.

But something inside her kept coming up empty. The more she tried to follow religious rules, the more she realized rules weren't helping her. So, she fought harder to get better at *more* rules. Out of her deeply unsettled spirit came impatience, over-reaction, judgment, and—she would later admit it—rage. She knew something had to change.

"What I was doing wasn't working," she once told me. "I was fighting for something I couldn't win. Grace."

One day she turned on a Phoenix-based Christian radio station, where the radio personality seemed to be speaking in a foreign language. Oh, it was *English*, all right. But this strange dialect described a generous God who lavishes His children with good gifts. It moved my mother-in-law to call the station to ask to meet with the radio personality.

The radio host agreed. And as they talked, he revealed a whole different way of approaching faith. At the host's urging, Lucy began searching for answers from one source she hadn't tried—the Bible. She shifted her focus from what she needed to do for God to what He had done for her. She joined a Bible study. She began to serve.

To hear my husband tell it, it was like Houdini himself showed up on the scene. Lucy went from rage-controlled to self-controlled. From fearful to hopeful. From judgmental to understanding.

She had tried for years to hustle her way into God's good graces, when all she needed to do was relax into God's good grace. This was the hinge on which her life turned.

It was a stunning transformation—so much so that my husband, then 18 years old, decided he wanted to be part of whatever—or whoever—had changed his mom. He gave his life to Jesus.

***

I stared out that big picture window in my mother-in-law's dining room. She chewed her food slowly. It gave us both time to think.

I remembered myself years earlier, when the just-the-facts journalist in me had wrestled with God. I didn't know whether He was real. No one could prove Him to me.

> **We believe that we are all saved the same way, by the undeserved grace of the Lord Jesus.**
>
> —ACTS 15:11 (NLT)

My boyfriend took me to breakfast one Sunday after church. My doubts about Christianity's claims were like the syrup I slathered onto my pancakes that morning: they covered everything and went deep.

"You just can't tell me God is real," I blurted.

Greg leaned across the table, took my hand, and said, "God is as real as if He's sitting right here with us. You want to know how I know? My mom had rage. And then she didn't anymore. It just stopped. Jesus calmed her spirit inside of her, just like *that*," he said, snapping his finger. His look was intense and sure. I have only seen that look one other time since—the day I walked down the aisle to marry him.

Lucy's story was the key that turned my own lock. I told God I didn't want to fight against Him anymore. I accepted the mystery of being saved by grace through faith.

Now I was holding my mother-in-law's hand much in the same way her son had held mine that day over pancakes. My

GOD'S GIFT OF HEARING
— Tez Brooks —

IN 2018 MISSIONARY Brother James was ministering among previously unreached Tibetan people. He met an old man who was deaf and decided to pray for him. After about ten minutes, the man's hearing came back completely. Brother James then shared the gospel with him. The old man, still in awe over his healing, said, "I wasn't born here. My parents died when I was young, so I was dropped here as a deaf orphan." James explained that God adopts anyone who follows Jesus. The man shouted, "Tell me about this God who healed me. I want to be His adopted child."

hand on top of hers. Her frail fingers gathered up under and into the strength of mine.

I wanted to tell her about the way her transformation had rippled into many lives, including mine. I wanted to tell her that only in my forties did I finally see how beautiful it is to come to God with my failures—and to watch Him redeem rather than rebuke them. She was in her forties when she figured that out too. I wanted so badly to compare notes.

I wanted to tell her that her big Italian persona had become a megaphone for God's grace. She was saved by it, and that's what changed her. She lived by it, and that's what changed others. And she never took credit for it, because she knew better.

But she was done with her food and ready for rest. None of us knew it yet, but that would be her last Mother's Day before God called her home.

I'd still like to compare notes. We all really miss her. I'm sure that in heaven she has yielded the center seat at the table to the One who deserves it—even though I'm equally sure that her big Italian persona is still pretty big. As big, at least, as the fullness of her understanding of God's grace.

A One-Star Review

Lynne Hartke

A superbloom year.

For weeks, rumors of a superbloom had dominated social media sites for Joshua Tree National Park (JTNP) in Southern California. I couldn't wait to experience the phenomenon—a rare time in the spring when a high number of wildflowers bloom after abundant rainfall and when the brown desert explodes in vibrant colors. The wildflowers had already begun blooming at our home in Chandler, Arizona—in the Sonoran Desert—but I wanted to experience it at JTNP, a place we had never visited before.

My husband, Kevin, and I decided to enter the park through the north entrance near Twentynine Palms, California. Our plan was to see the popular tourist sites before exiting the West Station. By doing so, we would spend most of our time in the Mojave Desert on the western half of the park. We planned to see all the beautiful wildflowers. Orange poppies. Yellow desert marigolds. Purple sand verbena. White dune primroses. Red chuparosa.

I couldn't wait!

But as we drove into the park, we didn't see a single blossom. Mile after mile, we encountered long stretches of nothing. Unless you counted the cactus. Everywhere I looked, I saw cactus.

Prickly pear cactus. Cholla cactus. Pencil cactus.

"If I wanted to see cactus," I grumped to Kevin, "I could have stayed home and walked out my front door."

"Maybe we are too early."

"But the flowers are blooming at home. The poppies and lupine are gorgeous already."

"We are at a higher elevation here."

"Really?" I dug out the tourist brochure the ranger had handed us at the entrance. *How had I missed that?* Sure enough, the elevation in this section of the park was over 3,000 feet, almost 2,000 feet higher than at home, creating a different habitat and ecosystem.

Spring flowers had not yet arrived.

Disappointed, we headed to Heart Rock, the first stop on my "Want to See" list. The ten-foot-high, heart-shaped stone rested on a flat space in a field of boulders, making it a perfect photo spot. An older gentleman took our pictures as we stood in front of the natural formation, even posing for a romantic kiss.

> **Then they despised the pleasant land; they did not believe his promise. They grumbled in their tents and did not obey the LORD.**
>
> —PSALM 106:24–25 (NIV)

"Thanks," we said, not bothering to check the photos before heading to Arch Rock, an impressive 30-foot expanse over another boulder field. From there we hiked around Jumbo Rocks, Skull Rock, and Split Rock. The fact that every tourist stop contained the word *rock* should have clued me into what we would be seeing. But social media posts of rainbows of colorful wildflowers had distorted my expectations.

"It's just a bunch of rocks," I complained to Kevin, as we headed to the car for a snack. Scrolling through my phone, I checked our photos.

"Oh no," I wailed.

"What happened?" Kevin questioned as he bit into an apple from the cooler.

"The man's thumb is in front of all our pictures at Heart Rock, even the kissing photo."

Kevin laughed, "He did seem a bit confused. Can you edit the pictures?"

"Maybe," I grumbled. I was not in the mood to be pacified. I rehearsed the disappointments of the day in my mind.

No flowers. Ruined photos. And it was cold!

I grabbed a granola bar and shuffled through our gear to find another layer to wear as I glared at the cloudy, overcast sky. The cold temperature matched my mood.

Frustrated, I sent our grown kids a text in our family group chat. "I can cross Joshua Tree National Park off my bucket list." I shivered as the chilly wind found a way down my neck. "I never need to come here again," I added.

"WHAT!" our youngest son, Zach, texted back. "I love that park." He couldn't fathom my negative response. He has spent several days here in the past, enjoying the scenery and rock climbing with his wife and friends. In fact, it was his exuberance that had convinced us to come, his stories of playing on the big groupings of rock boulders—like a natural jungle gym—and seeing the Milky Way in the evening in the park's dark sky zone.

Chastised, I examined my stinky attitude. I had often poked fun at the one-star reviews highlighted on social media sites of visitors who had been underwhelmed after encountering some of America's greatest beauty. I remember laughing in disbelief after reading a visitor's one-star review of Hawaii Volcanoes National Park because she couldn't touch the lava. Another person had whined about the Grand Canyon—one of the natural wonders of the world—as a large hole in the ground. And had also left a one-star review.

Assessing my heart, I had to admit I had become one of those underwhelmed reviewers. And even worse, I had become someone I loathe—a snarky tourist.

> **Do everything without grumbling or arguing, so that you may become blameless and pure.**
>
> **—PHILIPPIANS 2:14–15 (NIV)**

I needed an attitude adjustment.

I gathered up the granola bar wrappers from our snack and tossed them in a nearby trash can. I hoped my grumpy attitude would be as easily thrown away. I breathed a prayer. "Jesus, open my eyes to the beauty of this place."

As Kevin opened the map to plan our next stop at the park, I thought of the week before when I had watched our youngest granddaughter, Junie, age four. Her parents had barely walked out the door before she was rummaging through the craft supplies that I keep on hand for the grandkids.

Markers, glue sticks, crayons, construction paper, and stickers soon covered the coffee table in the living room as Junie created one masterpiece after another.

"Look, Grandma," she said again and again. "Look."

That day, watching her, I realized that part of the joy of the creation process is sharing the wonder of what you make with another person.

Now at Joshua Tree, the thought resurfaced again. Did God have things He made that He wanted to share with me? Had my unrealistic expectations blinded my eyes to the beauty right in front of me?

Kevin handed me the map, pointing out our options. "Do you want to see more of the park?" he asked warily, mindful of my negative attitude, "or do we push on toward the hotel?"

"Let's get more photos of the Joshua trees," I said, curious to discover what God had in store for us.

At closer examination, the Joshua trees proved to be fascinating. The spiky leaves and wayward branches reminded me of Dr. Seuss illustrations from my elementary-school readers. In fact, I learned the plants were not trees at all, but a species of yucca, with waxy, spiny leaves perfect for desert climate. We snapped photo after photo, capturing the whimsical trees from a variety of angles.

> "Has not my hand made all these things, and so they came into being?" declares the LORD.
>
> —ISAIAH 66:2 (NIV)

What else could I discover in this desert wonderland?

The rocks!

Arches. Hoodoos. Piles of boulders. Centuries ago, the once molten Monzogranite had pushed through the softer layer of surface rock. As the granite cooled and hardened, incredible cracks formed horizontally and vertically in the rock layers, leaving behind amazing jigsaw puzzles on the scrambled boulders throughout the park. Some layers appeared like hidden jewels, others like forgotten spines of prehistoric animals.

"Look at this! Look!" I exclaimed to Kevin, using the vernacular of our granddaughter.

Boulders. Joshua trees. Cactus. God had made a place of rare and unusual beauty. And imaginative! The park was a testimony to His incredible creative design.

"I can't wait to come back again," I said to Kevin as we loaded up the car to head out.

Kevin's eyebrows disappeared under the brim of his hat as he turned to stare at me. "Really?"

I nodded, not able to put it into words. I wanted to return to capture the sunrise over the unusual geological formations found here. I wanted to witness the dawn blooming across the park, like my joy had blossomed when I shifted my gaze to discover wonder.

By God's grace, even though we had seen no wildflowers, I *had* experienced a superbloom.

How to Rest in God's Presence

Tara Johnson

Thunder cracked, shaking the house and rattling the windows. I cringed. *No, no, no. There can't be a storm now.*

After a far-too-frustrating day, I had finally laid my four-year-old son, Nate, down for bed. His sisters were peacefully sleeping after a day of quarrels, spills, and messes. I just needed a break—a respite from screaming children, the frequent ringing of the phone, and barking dogs. I had spent my few precious free moments attempting to cross items off my to-do list, but failed. They were all good things, God-things related to ministry, but all my plans crumbled to ash as I darted from chaos to chaos, attempting to put out the fires that come from a young family.

And with every interruption, my irritation grew.

I had not-so-patiently waited for quiet, and now the storm threatened to undo all my hard work.

As silver illuminated the night sky, rain beat against the windows, and wind howled through the eaves, I heard a sound that caused my repressed irritation to bloom anew.

"Mama, stay?" My son's soft voice was a pleading whimper.

I heaved an exasperated sigh. There would be no way to finish my to-do lists tonight. As lightning flashed through my son's window, it illuminated the chubby curve of his cheeks and the sleepy blink of his big, brown eyes. My heart tugged.

"You need me to stay, buddy?"

He nodded as I padded to his bed and eased my weight onto his mattress, making myself as comfortable as I could on the tiny rectangle of space. I longed for my own blessedly soft pillow and adequately long bed, but I couldn't leave my little man while he was scared. Even as I settled in next to him, my mind began running through the enormous list of tasks I would have to accomplish the next day. My anxiety began to mount just at the thought of all that needed to be juggled.

And then it happened.

My son reached for my hand in the darkness, his eyes scrunched tight to shield his vision from the chaos shaking the house. The moment his chubby fingers brushed mine, he released a tight sigh. "Mama, you love me."

My chest constricted. I ran my fingers through his silky brown curls, wavering between overwhelming love for my little man and aggravation with myself.

I'm a messed-up mom. A mom who, even on my best days, tends to yell when I want to play it cool. I let my emotions spiral after teaching my kids how to trust God. I eat Nutella out of the jar when I intend to snack on carrot sticks. June Cleaver I'm not.

I moved my hand to stroke my son's back. "Do you need anything, honey? Water? Are you scared? Do you want to pray?"

Nate smiled sleepily. "Me just want you."

My heart thudded painfully in my chest. All my son wanted was me. No agenda. Just love and to sit in each other's presence. My previous irritation melted away. I hummed praise songs and stroked his soft curls as rain pelted the windows and thunder grumbled. And as I softly sang, my heart flooded with intangible peace. What could be better than this moment? This chance to love and praise and rest?

What if I had insisted on finishing my to-do list instead of comforting my son? I would have missed that sweet time of bonding. The quiet amid chaos.

And that's when I realized I had treated my relationship with God the same way. Sometimes we become angry with interruptions because we love our agendas and productivity more than we love the people in our lives. In the pursuit of "accomplish more," we lose the most precious gift

> Come to me, all you who are weary and burdened, and I will give you rest.
>
> —MATTHEW 11:28 (NIV)

of all: intimacy. The tricky thing about living in the cycle of go-go-go for so long is that after a while, the nonstop activity is like a drug. When it's gone, there's a terrifying hole of quiet that needs to be filled.

As I sat there, watching Nate slumber, I finally understood that I had traded time with Jesus for my checklists. Sure, I was doing work *for* God, but it wasn't the same as being close *to* God. The former is all about productivity. The latter is about relationship.

I've always wanted to be like Mary of Bethany because every time she was mentioned in Scripture, she ends up at the feet of Jesus. But how can I be like Mary if I refuse to be still? I fear too often I resemble Martha—frazzled, weary, and resentful.

Time with Jesus, sitting in His presence, must be sought for and fought for, because if we don't make it our priority to seek

Him, a thousand other things will crowd Him out. Productivity and performance are often the exact opposite of what God is wanting us to seek—Him.

From that sweet moment amid a raging storm and my son's sweet pleas for comfort, Jesus showed me interruptions are often divine appointments to stop and rest. To savor life. To enjoy times of intimacy that are too frequently put aside for "a more opportune time." If I truly want to be like Mary of Bethany and follow Him, it means He will interrupt my to-do lists and invite me to swap them for invitations to sit in His presence.

> "Martha, Martha," the Lord answered, "you are worried and upset about many things, but few things are needed— or indeed only one."
>
> —LUKE 10:41–42 (NIV)

How sad that many of us wait for a storm before He can catch our attention.

That night, I thought about Moses, one of my favorite people in the Bible. In Exodus 33, Moses had two requests of God: "Teach me your ways so I may know you..." and "If your Presence does not go with us, do not send us up from here" (Exodus 33:13, 15, NIV). More than anything, Moses longed to know God and stay in His Presence. If God wasn't in it, Moses didn't want it.

And God responded, "My Presence will go with you, and I will give you rest" (Exodus 33:14, NIV).

Rest. That's what I had been missing. I was doing all the right things, the godly to-do list, but I'd found no peace. No rest. The moment I stopped striving was the moment He stepped in and reminded me how sweet and gentle His love is.

Storms come and go, interruptions occur, and the best of well-laid plans crumble, but the love of the Father remains. Knowing Him is what matters. And when we love Him the way we should, loving others becomes easy.

Let the storm rage. All is well.

The Scarf

Nancie Carmichael

Can something frivolous spark faith?

It did for me last week, as I sat in the doctor's waiting room.

I was wearing Mom's scarf that day, the one made of fine wool with a tropical pattern of reds and blues and yellows. It's been in my possession since she's been gone, almost 30 years now. I ended it up with it because I gave it to her for her birthday 40 years ago. Mom loved pretty things, and I knew she could carry it off. Why a rancher's wife in northern Montana would have a thing for accessories is a mystery, but she sure did, and I inherited that from her.

I once heard a fashion expert say that we should never get rid of accessories. I took that advice to heart because my dresser drawers are full. Sometimes I forget about Mom's scarf and don't pull it out for a long time. Then, when I dig down to look for that pair of gloves or a shawl, there it is in the bottom drawer. And I slide its soft warmth around my neck.

I like wearing it when I'm not sure what to do, or how to respond to life, and I'm needing my mother. I immediately feel a little braver and stand a little taller. And honestly, sometimes I like it just for the splash of color. My mother was so spontaneous and fun.

This last week I'd had a series of doctor's appointments, as I'd not been feeling well. There were too many tests and procedures. Maybe it was the high blood pressure, the auto-immune condition, the unrelenting pain. There were no clear answers, but I just hadn't felt like my usual sparkling self. I felt more like a child who needed the comfort of her mother.

But the child's mother was long gone, and the time of childhood was over.

In the doctor's office, a young woman with blue hair and a clipboard asked me a few questions: "Are you afraid of falling in your home?"

I wanted to slug her with my handbag and retort, *What? Like when I'm doing hip-hop with my grands?* Instead, I meekly replied, "No," realizing I was now in the falling risk category. It was disconcerting, even as I tried to laugh it off.

> **Strength and honor are her clothing; she shall rejoice in time to come.**
>
> **—PROVERBS 31:25 (NKJV)**

The other day my five-year-old grandson, Conrad, patted my cheek and said, "Nana, your face is kinda squishy." *It's not just the face, Conrad.* There's a lot that's squishy, includ-ing my faith. Honestly, I don't mind getting older—it's quite wonderful when I consider my many blessings. But there are moments, like this one at the doctor's office, when there's pain and uncertainty. When I'm reminded of my mortality.

As I waited for the doctor to come in, I held the scarf to my face and whispered in my thoughts: *Mom? This is a hard part of the journey. You never told me about this. You never complained. After Dad died, you journeyed on even though you had cancer, just like him. You were so brave and optimistic. Still teaching Bible study, still driving to see your kids. Still showing up with your funny self, dressing up like a bag lady and going to my sister's garage sale to surprise her. Inviting in a Fuller Brush salesman to watch the end of the Trailblazer game with you because it was so close, and you wanted to watch it with somebody. You could be a little bit crazy, but how I loved your spontaneity, your laughter. How I miss you.*

I'm still here, with all the goodness and hardness of life. Your child is aging. What do you think of that? There have been many losses, and everything feels harder now.

> ## So then faith comes by hearing, and hearing by the word of God.
>
> **—ROMANS 10:17 (NKJV)**

I held Mother's scarf and listened, waiting to hear some ennobling thoughts. Encouraging words. Where and what is my purpose now? What do I hold on to? Where is my strength?

The doctor came into the examination room, and it turned out to be an encouraging visit as she gave helpful advice about medication, diet, and lifestyle. But I knew my biggest underlying condition was my wavering faith. Does God really care? Is He there for us, all through life? Sure, in the blessings, but what about in pain and loss and disillusionment?

As I drove home, I thought back to when I was 16, and Mom and I were doing dishes. I blurted out to her that I didn't believe there was a God. Terrible things were happening in the world. Vietnam. I was learning about the Holocaust, about racial injustice. How could there be a God? Mother put down her dish towel and looked at me with her smiling brown eyes:

"Of course there's a God. And it's OK that you're questioning it. He's always been there for me, and He'll always be there for you. Now, let's get these dishes done."

GOD'S GIFT OF SMELL

— Lynne Hartke —

THE ELEPHANT TREE, *Bursera microphylla,* is a rare, protected tree in Arizona, Southern California, and Mexico. These trees can survive a year without rain by storing water in their short, fat trunks. The tree is recognizable by its peeling white bark, purple berries, red sap, and tiny, fernlike leaves. The crushed leaves have a strong fragrance reminiscent of frankincense, a scent that clings to anyone who brushes against the branches. The elephant tree is an example of what followers of Jesus should do—leave a pleasing aroma on everyone with whom they come in contact.

I don't remember what else we talked about that day, or even what we did, but her calm response held me for years as I wondered, *What makes her so sure?* My beautiful mother had a sturdy faith, and it came from knowing God by reading the Bible, by a life of prayer. Her life was not easy, but she knew how much she needed Him. Eventually, her contagious, joy-filled example convinced me to trust, too, and as a young woman, I made that initial step into faith.

That day, as I drove home from the doctor's office in a place of pain and uncertainty, my mother's memory filled me. It hit me all over again—how much I need Jesus. Even in places of pain and uncertainty, He is there—the same, yesterday, today, and forever, offering His grace and presence in all journeys.

Right there in the car, I chose to trust Him again. I prayed, *Lord, I'm in. No matter what.*

After I got home, I put Mom's scarf away, feeling somehow reassured. Sometimes the smallest things remind of us what we know. Indeed, God has been there for me throughout life.

> **Jesus Christ is the same yesterday and today and forever.**
>
> —HEBREWS 13:8 (NIV)

Paul wrote to Timothy, "You must continue in the things which you have learned and been assured of, knowing from whom you have learned them, and that from childhood you have known the Holy Scriptures, which are able to make you wise for salvation through faith which is in Christ Jesus" (2 Timothy 3:14–15, NKJV).

Continue.

It was time to continue in the faith.

Beautiful, timeless faith like the comforting caress of a soft, warm scarf, reminding me through the vibrant colors that the joy of the Lord is my strength, no matter what the day holds.

Granna Goes to Camp

Joni Topper

You're too old for this. That was my first thought when my church youth group asked me to take them to camp. At sixty-three, I was still active, walking often and not shying away from physical tasks. Still, going to camp for five days in the Texas summer heat with a group of fourteen- and fifteen-year-olds felt like a stretch. The hilly terrain and outdoor events required strength in your legs and stamina in your "want to."

My "want to" was my family. My grandchildren, Brooks and Oliver, would be there, and two other members of the group, Bartley and Jackson, were Brooks's friends. Getting to know the kids Brooks hung around with on a daily basis incentivized me. I also looked forward to building a stronger relationship with the fifth member of our youth group, Shelby.

Another motivation was the chance to get to know Oliver, who had been grafted into my family only months before when my son and his mom got married. He struggled to feel like part of the family. With a huge chapter of shared experiences between us missing, bonding with him had been slow and tedious. I hoped that by spending time with my new grandson, we would transition into full-family mode.

Oliver had received a guitar the Christmas before camp. He brought his instrument to youth Bible study every week. Although my guitar skills were weak, I could play enough for him to follow my lead. The teens loved music so much that they often asked if we could extend class time in order to sing more. Oliver and I were planning to play together at camp too. Shelby was interested in playing along with us, and she had borrowed my extra guitar so she could experiment with it. She decided against it and planned to return my instrument so that I could bring it to camp, because I did not want to take my good guitar to that setting. But then...

> **The Lord is my strength and my shield; my heart trusted in Him, and I am helped; therefore my heart greatly rejoices, and with my song I will praise Him.**
>
> —PSALM 28:7 (NKJV)

"Oh no, I forgot the guitar!" Shelby lugged her sleeping gear and bag from her mom's car and hobbled across the parking lot on her walking cast. I'd been amazed that she was willing to go to youth camp as the only girl in a group of four boys. But I should not have been surprised, since a foot injury and a walking cast hadn't discouraged her.

There was no time for Shelby to go home and retrieve the guitar. This meant that Oliver would offer the only accompaniment for our group devotional time. He would have to learn quickly how to lead—if he had the courage to go it alone. I knew it wouldn't be easy, especially in front of a group of his peers.

Once we arrived and Shelby and I had settled into the girls' dorm, another small church adopted us as their family for the week. Their leader and the girls made Shelby feel right at home.

My brief anxious moment about her not having another female teenager to hang out with evaporated.

Brooks brought a spirit of cooperation to everything we did. The boys were not shy about selecting different activities. One chose archery, another basketball, while another joined in with field games. They all had the confidence to go their own way sometimes, while other times they chose to play games together, even taking on some older serious athletes on the basketball court. They impressed me with their wide variety of choices.

Oliver disregarded all the sporting activities of the week. He just wanted to sit somewhere with his guitar and experiment with chords and rhythms. With his music in hand, he required few other social interactions.

Each of the teens felt free to choose their own activities during the day. My rule—we would all stand in line together for meals. The twenty-minute lines gave us ample time to get caught up on what we'd been doing.

While we stood there together, I learned about these kids' personalities. Bartley, who stood over six feet tall and had never met a stranger, made a new friend at every meal every day. His magnetic personality entertained us all. In fact, our entire entourage made friends with Bartley's lunch-line girlfriends.

Jackson, one of my grandson's classmates, maintained the role of "the quiet one" in our group. People stopped and listened when he spoke in his deep commanding voice. During devotions, his knowledge of Scripture showed us his grounded nature. His calm presence made my grandmother's heart happy that my grandson had chosen him as a close friend.

There were bonding times outside of the lunch line too. One morning Shelby and I walked down to the water and sat for a while enjoying the overcast sky and watching the breeze blow across the lake. Our words were few because the beauty of the day did not require words.

The camp enlisted an adult man from another church to watch over my boys in their dorm. The man who accepted that challenge offered a kind spirit. Oliver amazed him. "Everyone in our dorm listens to him when he plays the guitar. They're amazed that he's only been playing for a few months. I'm amazed at his steady, intentional commitment to his guitar."

> **Trust in the LORD with all your heart, and lean not on your own understanding.**
>
> **—PROVERBS 3:5 (NKJV)**

Despite the praise, Oliver struggled with his self-confidence and the difficulties of playing for his peers. After evening worship our church group huddled in a gazebo for small-group devotionals. Since we only had one guitar, Oliver led by himself for the first time. The kids were kind to him, but he felt conspicuous. After his first attempt, he decided he would not bring his guitar out again.

On the third evening we were there, after worship and devotionals, the camp hosted a big event on the field. Lights, colored powder bombs, laughter, and races pierced the still night air. Oliver approached me as I stood watching the teams laugh and emerge from the powder bombs tinted like balloons escaping into the night. He put his arm around my shoulder. "Granna, why is it so hard?"

"What?" I asked.

"Playing for them to sing. I know how to play, but it's hard to lead by myself."

"Oh, Oliver, everything you ever do that is important will be hard. Just ask God to help you. He will." We talked a little more, but mostly we just stood together with his arm around my shoulder, watching the bursts of color and listening to the laughter.

I had convinced myself to go to camp in part because I prayed it would offer me an opportunity to spend time getting to know this new grandchild of mine. In that summer night air, we bonded. Oliver braved bringing his guitar out again the next time we gathered for devotionals, and I witnessed him face a difficult part of growing up with courage.

By the end of the week, the kids had shared a musical moment. They joined the band on stage and sang their hearts out as though they performed on a regular basis. Oliver, having grown by pushing through his frustrations, joined the others there.

Driving home, I counted my blessings: Brooks, Oliver, Bartley, Jackson, and Shelby. The next few years I enjoyed these young people even more because of the relationships we formed at camp. My heart swelled with appreciation that I'd gotten to know them. Those few days at camp gave me a glimpse into who these burgeoning young people were becoming. The experience reminded me that in saying yes to opportunities God offers—like going to camp when you think you are too old to go—we receive the very best gifts ourselves.

Finding Joy in Alzheimer's

Miriam Green

The first time she cried in my arms, I was overcome with emotion. Mom's Alzheimer's was advancing, and I found myself thrust into the role of mothering my own mother. I remember fervently pleading with God to change the diagnosis: *God, I demanded angrily, bring my mother back to me!* As the Mishnah, a collection of Jewish oral traditions, wisely states, "If one prays for something that has already passed, this constitutes a prayer in vain." Wrestling with this idea, I embarked on a journey to accept our new reality. Could I still find moments of joy amid the challenges of Mom's diagnosis? I made it my mission to uncover the hidden blessings in this heartbreaking situation.

Finding joy in the midst of Alzheimer's is like shining a beacon of light in a pitch-black room to reveal the hidden treasures within. It's a conscious decision to seek joy, because, let's face it, Alzheimer's is a devastating disease. Witnessing a loved one slowly fade away fills your heart with an unrelenting sense of loss.

My mom, Naomi Cohen, received her Alzheimer's diagnosis more than 12 years ago. I was ill-prepared for the turmoil Alzheimer's introduced into our lives. I didn't grasp that every emotion I displayed would be magnified in Mom's behavior. It took time for me to realize that Mom had entered an alternate reality. I constantly reminded myself that it wasn't her fault; angry outbursts, panic attacks, and the slow erasing of her memories were all being caused by the disease.

In such circumstances, I could have given up and labeled Mom as "sick," placing her in a memory care facility. Instead, I chose a different path—one of rediscovery and compassion. I aimed to look past the veil of this disease to reconnect with the mother I knew was still within her and to fill Mom's days with love, laughter, and music.

I learned that when in doubt, the best solution is to sing. We know that music resonates with the Alzheimer's-afflicted brain, so I made sure to know all the songs Mom loved. Despite my questionable singing abilities, I belted out those tunes with enough enthusiasm to coax Mom into singing along. And she had an incredible voice.

> **My body and mind fail; but God is the stay of my mind, my portion forever.**
>
> **—PSALM 73:26 (JPS)**

Picture this intimate scene: Mom tentatively undressing for a shower, with me serving as her personal coach. I give her instructions. "That's right, take off your nightgown." "This is soap; you rub it on your body to clean your skin." "Oh, the towel stays here, not in the shower. We want it to stay dry."

As the water reached the perfect temperature, I started to sing. "I'm gonna wash that man right out of my hair." Before you knew it, we were having a singing fest in the bathroom. Mom forgot her fear of the water as singing distracted her, allowing her to shower with joy.

I learned to improvise and go with the flow. One day Mom had a doctor's appointment, and it fell on me to get her there on time. The preparation process was an unpredictable adventure. We needed to eat breakfast, get dressed, put on shoes, a coat, and a hat. We had to leave the house with enough time to accommodate our leisurely walking pace.

Never mind that Mom placed a cookie in her mug instead of a tea bag or cut her toast with a knife and fork or poured juice into her cereal and milk. Her clothes lay neatly on the bed, but when I returned after a brief absence, she was dressed in three pairs of underwear, two skirts, and mismatched shoes. How did I persuade Mom to dress more appropriately without causing frustration or anger? Rational explanations rarely worked. Instead, I embraced humor and distraction. I might drum my fingers on the dressing table to the tune of the "William Tell Overture," and Mom inevitably joined in. Laughter ensued, and in that moment of fun, I seized the opportunity to re-dress her, put her shoes on, place her hat on her head, hand her a bag to hold, and we were out the door.

One tried and true outing that always put a smile on Mom's face was when we attended synagogue together. The prayers and tunes of my childhood continued to soothe and engage her long after her understanding of the service faded. There was comfort in repetition, and in the easy hellos my friends bestowed on her after services.

My observance of Jewish ritual anchored me throughout our journey. When I first started making challah bread each Friday night, I would say a blessing over every ingredient. Most of the blessings were focused on being a mom to my children, and how I could turn those blessings into a force for good in raising caring, passionate individuals.

When sifting flour: *Please, God, help me sift out of my life what is not necessary to my inner being.*

When adding sugar: *God, bring to the fore what is good and sweet within me so that I may express those emotions to my beloved family.*

When adding salt: *God, grant me the determination to set the appropriate boundaries in my life.*

The one blessing that spoke to me the most was always the one over the yeast: *Dear God, give me creativity in raising my children as this yeast raises the humble wheat into an extraordinary loaf of bread.*

One Friday morning as I was preparing my challah dough, I realized that these blessings could equally apply to my taking care of Mom. I needed strength, sweetness, and creativity to channel our interactions into meaningful and caring moments. I needed the brightness, the *ma'or panim*—a term that means "bright face," referring to the moment when the person in front of you sees you, but is also associated with adding oil to my dough—to treat every individual with the respect they deserved. The tasks involved in creating bread were there to guide me to a heightened awareness of God's involvement in my life and in my treatment of those I loved, even as those relationships changed.

> # She is clothed with strength and splendor; she looks to the future cheerfully.
>
> **—PROVERBS 31:25 (JPS)**

Another lesson came when I recited the grace after meals one day after eating a sandwich at Mom's house. "May the Merciful One bless my parents, my teachers…"

Throughout my upbringing, Mom had imparted countless lessons, some practical (like how to inspect eggs in a carton before purchase), and others more profound (such as the importance of loving your children unconditionally). She consistently radiated optimism about the future. Was Mom still my teacher? Did Alzheimer's rob her of this role too?

Yes, I realized, Mom was still my teacher. She was teaching me to use my creativity and my compassion to love her entirely. She was teaching me that even in difficult moments, there was hope for redemption.

Finding the positive aspects of Mom's behavior and the life she lives despite her limitations is undoubtedly challenging. We are acutely aware that Alzheimer's will eventually claim all of her. In my darker moments, tears flow for the impending loss of my beloved mother. But, with God's love and gentle presence in my life, I have learned to accept her transformation from my savvy, cheerful, competent mother into the sweet, simple woman who struggles to remember who I am. The number of times we sit together in the same café or stroll past the same stores is inconsequential. What truly matters is that we are together. I cherish those moments of sheer joy and laughter as much as she does.

Transformation is a process, and as life happens there are tons of ups and downs. It's a journey of discovery—there are moments on mountaintops and moments in deep valleys of despair.

—Rick Warren

CHAPTER 6

Journeys of Faith

Just the Two of Us

Roberta Messner

It was the old, rusted glider that did it. Passing time in a doctor's waiting room, I reached for one of the old magazines that seems to show up in such places. I knew the cover well. In better times, on my weekends off from nursing, I'd written features for them and arranged the spaces for the accompanying photo shoots. I'd styled that porch. Picked the flowers in the white ironstone pitcher from the lady's cutting garden. Arranged confections on vintage pedestals. Fluffed pillows in a glider that time had once forgotten.

Then the publisher fell on hard times and shuttered its doors. So did I. I'd taken a horrible fall and struck my face. Tumors that burned like a fiery griddle—once in remission—returned with a vengeance, requiring seven surgeries.

"Change Your Before into an After," my story's bold, black letters promised. Words I'd written when I believed such things were possible. That a creaky, rusty glider past its prime could be the centerpiece for a family starting over.

I turned the pages to my words and to the life I'd left far behind. Once upon a time, my Before and After features had become a reader favorite. An incorrigible junker, I combed the hills and hollows of my home state of West Virginia for the stuff nobody wanted. I saw potential in everything, and I carted all of it back to my 120-year-old log cabin to rehab.

Then my life took a turn not worthy of glossy magazine pages. In intractable pain from facial and mouth tumors, and addicted to prescription opioids, *I* was the one in need of rehab.

I did everything I could to try to turn my life around. But I was no match for this enemy. I learned that a broken-down person's Before and After wasn't as easy as the objects I transformed. God was the only one to turn to. It took an absolute miracle to turn me around, and that's exactly what happened. On April 1, 2018, He delivered me from the chains that had bound me. I never again took as much as an aspirin for tumor pain. It was gone. I never thought of those opioids again.

But now the cabin I adored was practically falling down around me. I'd lost the order, comfort, and beauty of my beloved home. It was a Before with no After. Hopeless junk cluttered every nook and cranny of what was once a place of peace. Discards as broken as I was accused me at every turn. The person

> **Therefore, if anyone is in Christ, the new creation has come. The old has gone, the new is here!**
>
> **—2 CORINTHIANS 5:17 (NIV)**

who once saw possibility and lived a life of creativity no longer existed. But where does a home décor stylist go to tell the truth? I'd held it together pretty well during better times, but my pristine façade was quickly crumbling. And that day in the doctor's office, staring at the glider that I'd made the centerpiece of a family's hope for a better After, I knew something had to change.

Battle-hardened from the struggle, in the middle of a long, restless night, I turned it over to God. *I'm all alone, Lord, and*

I can't do this by myself. You know what I need, my limited resources, my future, my dreams.

I had a friend who knew the depths of my struggle. She and her husband flipped houses, so a mess didn't scare her. And she was practical. Budget-wise. Knew the dire straits I was in from medical debt. "This stuff would bring a pretty penny," she said. "If you sold it, you could hire someone to help you get your home back again."

Another friend knew just the person to enlist. Jenn, a young woman who'd once been a contractor, could do anything, and wasn't afraid of hard work. What convinced me was her history of opioid addiction. She'd lost it all and was trying to get her own life back. Like me.

Jenn and I hit it off instantly. She was a six-wick candle of light who understood where I'd been, how I longed to imagine a new life. And she was fun and funny. When the mess overwhelmed me, she called from a ladder: "Ahh, Berta! Home wasn't built in a day. Or was that Rome?"

We cleared the cabin of everything. The clutter I'd accumulated when taking care of the cabin got to be too much. Sold and consigned the pretentious antiques and collectibles until the interior and its glistening log walls were like a fresh canvas you could paint your life on.

Jenn didn't just work tirelessly; she "got" me. We were telling a new story, how nothing is ever broken and battered beyond repair. Jenn was drawn to the forsaken furnishings I'd snagged for my Before and After features but never got around to. Wanted to know the where and when and how of every find. "South side on trash day," I told her about a pair of vintage wing chairs. "Yep. Kicked to the curb. Of course, I hauled them home." In a box of old linens we found yardage of old floral bark cloth and other retro fabrics. Just like that, a plan and a dream began to turn discards into something of value. Relentless regrets replaced with joy and, yes, even gratitude.

We went off to the garage, dragging in a seen-better-days pie safe and a church pew with luscious layers of color that included someone's carved initials. "A kid got bored during a sermon," Jenn said wryly.

Nah! The pew told a story of redemption; I felt it in my very bones. "That was someone who went to the altar," I said. In that moment, my little cabin seemed as sacred as a cathedral, my heart a kneeling bench.

Joining them was a farm table with worn and wonderful shades of white. My thoughts took me back to Texas, where I'd scouted homes for potential magazine articles. I attended an antique

> # Forget the former things; do not dwell on the past.
>
> —ISAIAH 43:18 (NIV)

show out in a field where I'd spotted a similar table I'd thought would work if I could refurbish it.

"Oh, honey!" the vendor had said in her Southern drawl. "We can't ever get rid of a table's *storrrry*."

Affirmation! As if we needed it. We gathered up a homey mismatch of chairs to set around my has-been table. They were as quirky and full of purpose as *I* was beginning to feel.

What I needed was all around me. If it had heart, I called it art. Old quilts, coverlets, and pillows uncovered in forgotten boxes added softened-by-time coziness. It seemed they'd been waiting to be rediscovered. When we hung wool tartan blankets that were given to veterans returning home from war on wooden pegs, I could hardly get the words out past the lump in my throat. "Is it just me, Jenn? This place almost seems to hug me."

Jenn smoothed a rag rug over the heart pine floor. One look at the twitch of her mouth and I knew a laugh was coming. "I feel it too," she said. "So did the guy who came to work on the furnace the other day." Who could forget him, wearing that *Too Cold at Home* sweatshirt? "He got a call for another job," Jenn went on. "I heard him say, 'I'm at the cabin. I'm getting that "I don't want to leave" feeling.'"

I feel the same way. It's the place where grace came to stay. Shelters me. Where the simplest pleasures and everyday blessings follow one another like pearls on a string. If you listen closely, you might think the cabin is talking to itself. Or that maybe it's me. I'm not the only one who lives here, so I might be chatting with God. Praying, which is easy to do here. Recounting that old, old story of redemption that never gets old. The story that restores the beautifully broken to tell a new story. Turns the mistakes and messes of our Befores into an Everafter.

My Pioneer Journey

Glenda Ferguson

"I finally made it to the hotel," I announced over the phone to my husband, Tim, back home in Indiana.

Tim asked how my car trip had been to northern Illinois.

"No trouble. Just seemed to take a long time."

We talked about tomorrow's itinerary into Wisconsin and promised to talk again in two days. Right before hanging up, Tim said, "You're on your way. Love you!"

I sure didn't feel like I was on my way. It was the first day of a 6-week summer trip tracing the footsteps of pioneer Laura Ingalls Wilder through the Midwest. The beloved author of the Little House on the Prairie books had inspired millions with her tales of growing up on the frontier and the challenges her family had faced along the way. After teaching for 10 years, I had searched for a project that would revive my career and discovered the Teacher Creativity Fellowship, which provides money for educators to seek out new experiences to help support their classroom work. At the urging of my school colleagues, I applied, with the idea of traveling alone to the prairie, museums, and homesites of the famous author.

Then the most frightening thing happened: I won the fellowship. I was the first from my district to receive such an honor, and I reveled in all the publicity and accolades. Before I could consider all the consequences, I booked my hotel rooms, packed my suitcases, and headed out. Though it was daunting to be on my own, I felt certain that God was guiding me toward this journey, and the ladies of my church, my prayer warriors, assured me of their constant vigilance.

I was excited, but also anxious. In those days before the internet and GPS, I had to rely on paper maps to navigate the unfamiliar terrain. I fretted about my driving abilities and doubted my navigational skills. Even Tim didn't know my true feelings.

Even though I usually went to bed early, I didn't feel like turning in yet, and besides, my nerves were shot from the long drive. Instead of following my nighttime routine of journaling and reading a devotional, I unfolded the Wisconsin map and studied it until my vision blurred from squinting at the highway numbers and the exits, hoping I would know which way to turn. When I did climb into bed late that evening, I tossed around on my mattress like I was inside a covered wagon traveling down a bumpy road.

The next morning I raised my exhausted body out of bed. Part of me wanted to turn around, but I would disappoint so many people if I didn't finish this trip. My fourth-grade students looked forward to the postcards I would be sending them. My mom anticipated viewing the photos I would snap. Most of all, I would be letting myself down. This trip was a leap of faith and a challenge that I needed to accomplish.

After navigating and constantly checking road signs, I arrived in Pepin, Wisconsin, Laura's birthplace, without finding pleasure in the scenery along the way. I spent the rest of the day exploring the museum and the small replica cabin in the area that used to be known as the Big Woods. After buying some postcards, I flopped down at a picnic table, so tired from my sleepless night that I could barely stay awake, and wrote messages to my students.

At the post office, the friendly postmaster, curious about my trip, said, "You must be so excited to do this for your class. I can just bet that they will treasure those postcards." I slunk out of there quickly. The postal worker displayed more enthusiasm about my trip than I did.

Something had to change. But there was no time to think about it. I needed to focus while navigating to Minnesota, to the museum commemorating Laura Ingalls Wilder's family homestead at Plum Creek, near the town of Walnut Grove, Minnesota. Laura's life there was the basis for her book *On the Banks of Plum Creek*, and it was the setting for the hit TV series *Little House on the Prairie*.

> **The Lord himself goes before you and will be with you; he will never leave you nor forsake you. Do not be afraid; do not be discouraged.**
>
> **—DEUTERONOMY 31:8 (NIV)**

I checked into my reserved room, which would be my base camp for the next two days. Then I began unfolding the map for the road to Plum Creek. I stopped myself. Every pioneer knew the importance of getting a good night's sleep. That evening I followed my nightly routine. In my journal, I wrote about the events of the day and confessed my anxiety. Before I grabbed my devotional off the nightstand, I noticed the front cover of the hotel's directory. It had an inspirational quote: *Every accomplishment, no matter how large or small, first began with the thought "I think I can."* All my life I had struggled with confidence in my own abilities. Usually the negative messages of "I can't" won. I just knew God had drawn my attention to this cover. A brief message with a profound meaning for me.

The next morning I felt rested for the Plum Creek trip. As I parked at the site, I noticed plum trees still thriving along the banks, and the creek flowing just as clear as during Laura's time. I did what any pioneer would do in the middle of July. I removed my shoes and waded in. The chilly water jolted me wide awake. This spot turned into an oasis from the heat and the swirling thoughts in my head.

A family with two young children joined me in the shallow stream. All of us started laughing for the sheer joy of a dip in the cool water on a summer day. For me, the wonder of being in this location, just as it had been described in Laura's stories, revived my spirit.

That night I called Mom, my biggest cheerleader. After I described her favorite area, she said, "You will have to bring me lots of photos. I want to feel like I was in that creek too." She also passed along a message from my grandma: "I have angels watching over you as you travel."

Even with all the positive messages and prayers, my nervousness occupied my thoughts in the dark. I fretted about my driving abilities. Suppose I got lost? What if my car broke down in the middle of nowhere? I was headed for a panic attack. A Bible verse came to my mind, a verse that Laura Ingalls Wilder relied on as she traveled. I grabbed my Bible and found Deuteronomy 31:8. I personalized it, turning it into a prayer: "The Lord himself goes before Glenda and will be with Glenda; he will never leave Glenda nor forsake Glenda. Do not be afraid; do not be discouraged, Glenda." I repeated that verse over and over until I calmed down my breathing. God was with me.

The next day I scheduled a tour of the museum, which was located in a church. Months ago, I had ordered posters and books from the gift shop. Rosalie, an employee, had included a personal note in the package and extended an invitation for a tour when I was in Minnesota. As soon as I arrived, Rosalie led me through the church and recounted many of the trials that Laura and the Ingalls family had survived. She gave me a list of Laura's favorite Scripture readings, including Psalm 121:7–8, which Laura marked for safe travels: "The LORD will keep you from all harm—he will watch over your life; the LORD will watch over your coming and going both now and forevermore" (NIV). Even though Rosalie and I only just met, I felt like I had bonded with a special friend.

I left there with a new boldness and continued my journey to South Dakota, where Laura's Pa and Ma finally settled down and where she would marry Almanzo Wilder. As I traveled, I reflected on my own family. Most of my family, especially my parents and grandparents, were born and stayed in the same small town. I often heard them discuss their desire to visit the faraway places they read about in books, but they never carried through on it. I was the first to graduate from college and move to another state—and now I was the first woman in our family to travel alone. During this journey I had gained confidence in doing

> **Neither height nor depth, nor anything else in all creation, will be able to separate us from the love of God that is in Christ Jesus our Lord.**
>
> **—ROMANS 8:39 (NIV)**

GOD'S GIFT OF HEARING
— Buck Storm —

I CLOSE MY eyes and listen. Paws pad on the rug. A car passes outside.

I listen harder. Leaves tap the window. I hear the breath of wind that moves them.

Sometimes we need to turn off one sense to better experience others. It's easy to tumble along in the information deluge that defines much of our day. Sometimes God will shout through the roar, but other times His is the softest whisper. I suspect this is calculated. He wants me to block the nonsense and focus on the real, the meaningful, the truth.

I want that too.

I close my eyes and listen.

---

what the pioneers had done: navigating, setting up "camp," and exploring new sites. I realized that this journey could be a fresh start for me just as it had been for Laura's family. Only through God's grace could I have come this far.

Outside of Independence, Kansas, on a cloudy morning, I arrived at the popular location of the little house on the prairie. This was the site where Laura and her family had lived before settling at Plum Creek, and while Laura was still a toddler when they lived in Kansas, her family's memories were the basis for her book *The Little House on the Prairie*. Unlike Plum Creek, you can see a reproduction of the Ingalls' original homestead, and it remains a popular tourist destination. As the clouds cleared away, I marveled at how blue the sky was. Visitors strolled through the area all day. I longed for the quiet that wide-open spaces could bring, so I returned after closing.

As I stepped out of my car, the warm breeze ruffled my hair. Fragrant wildflowers of yellow, blue, purple, and white swayed in the prairie grass. Songbirds belted out their tunes signaling the end of the day. I took a deep cleansing breath and imagined settling in this land as a pioneer. In this secluded location, where I should have experienced isolation, I felt as if God stood right beside me.

> **The LORD will keep you from all harm—he will watch over your life.**
>
> **—PSALM 121:7 (NIV)**

I completed my journey at Laura's forever home at Rocky Ridge Farm in Mansfield, Missouri. It was here, wrapping up an amazing journey, that I realized this trip had not been just about checking off the sites I visited. This trip transformed my trust in God. He revealed His presence with each step of my pioneer journey through kind strangers, encouragement from my family, and the influence of His natural world. I discovered I could trust God in all circumstances.

Now, back home in Indiana, I pray, "What journey is next for this pioneer?"

Forever Changed by
Divine Encounters

Christel Owoo

Approaching the end of my university studies in the Netherlands,
I prepared for my master's thesis research project in Ghana.
Being a student, I didn't have the finances for the four-month
academic trip. Following the advice of my supervisor, I applied
for funds from several organizations and requested twice the
money I needed, as they typically only give half. Because at
that time I was not a Christian, I sought institutes that had a
nonreligious requirement for eligibility. Much to my surprise,
every institution replied with a positive response and granted
me exactly what I had requested, doubling the amount I
needed.

In July 1994, close to my twenty-fifth birthday, I reached
Kumasi, Ghana's second-largest city, and checked into my small,
dim room at a Presbyterian guesthouse. A sense of homesickness
consumed me as I struggled with where to begin my research.
Because my focus was on how Western cultures perceived non-
Western culture, I decided that visiting a local tourist attraction
might be a good way to start understanding local culture. I
grabbed my newly acquired tourist guidebook and went out to
look for the sword of Okomfo Anokye, one of the founders of
the Ashanti empire. I couldn't find my way, so I approached a man

walking in the same direction as me and asked for help. He said he would take me to the place, but only if I promised to listen while we walked together. I agreed—something I regretted later. To my boredom and frustration, he spoke about eternal life all the way to the spot. I kept my promise, as I was a woman of firm principles, although I didn't want to hear what he was saying. At the destination, he said he did not know why I wanted to see that place, but he had kept his promise and brought me. I stared into a dark hole in the ground—the place where the legendary sword is said to be buried, now covered with a stone marker—leaving me unsure of my reason for being there. I turned to the man, only to find out he had disappeared. Dissatisfaction took over, and I made my way back to the guesthouse.

But that was only the first of many strange encounters with Christians throughout my time in Ghana. Back in the guesthouse, a young visiting

> He saved us, not on the basis of deeds which we did in righteousness, but in accordance with His mercy, by the washing of regeneration and renewing by the Holy Spirit.
>
> —TITUS 3:5 (NASB)

pastor approached me and quoted a scripture. He said, "If your hand or foot causes you to sin, cut it off and throw it away. It's better to enter eternal life with only one hand or one foot than to be thrown into eternal fire with both of your hands and feet." What was he thinking? *I am not a sinner!* Irritated by such an insolent statement, I brushed him off.

Some days later, the in-house Presbyterian pastor invited me to his church.

"I am not a Christian," I replied. "My parents didn't raise me that way."

"But you are of age," he pointed out. "You can make your own decisions."

Speechless, I knew he was right—I couldn't hide behind my parents' decision. Especially since I considered myself an independent, strong-willed woman. How could I depend on other people's choices for me? This conversation lingered in the back of my head and left me with a sense of uncertainty.

Eventually I attended a service at his church, but not because of his invitation—oh no! I wouldn't do anything anyone told me to do! My church visit was strictly for academic reasons. As part of my cultural research, I decided to investigate the high church attendance among Ghanaians. However, after the service I noticed a sense of peace inside me—a feeling I hadn't known before. It piqued my curiosity, so I kept returning to church.

After one of those services, a young woman my age pulled me to the front row. With a bright smile, she gently pushed me to sit beside her and turned her face to me. She said, "Jesus is my friend."

I was stunned. How could Jesus be her friend? He was not alive, if indeed He had ever been alive. There must be something wrong with her. But I had come to know her through previous church visits, and she was smart, funny, and sane. No, nothing was wrong with her mind. I was confused—she seemed so sure. Even after I left the service, I couldn't shake the idea of "Jesus is my friend" from my mind.

In September a British man, Mark, arrived at the guesthouse. It gave me a sense of familiarity, having a European nearby. We had just become acquainted when Mark became seriously ill and was admitted to a small clinic. In Ghana back then, not having family around meant being isolated in a hospital. I assumed the responsibility of visiting him twice daily and providing assistance whenever possible.

During my first visit, Mark needed my help to read his Bible for him, as he was too sick to read. For the first time in my life, I read the Bible. I don't remember the words I read, but it must have been about Jesus's baptism, as Mark meditated aloud regarding a dove coming down. I found it all strange but helped the sick man anyway.

On a different occasion, as I washed him, he suddenly asked me to stop as he got a revelation. He said God showed him that in the same way as he can't wash himself, but needs my help, he can't wash himself from sin but needs God's help to wash away his sin. It was the only thing he said, but I could see it affected him. It planted deep in me the truth of that one sentence—as a seed that would bear fruit, eventually.

Two weeks later, when his health didn't improve, an emergency plane flew him from Kumasi back to the UK. At the airport

> **And everyone who has given up houses or brothers or sisters or father or mother or children or property, for my sake, will receive a hundred times as much in return and will inherit eternal life.**
>
> —MATTHEW 19:29 (NLT)

he handed me his Bible and said it was precious to him, but he wanted me to have it. It became the first Bible I read for myself.

As October arrived, it was time for me to return to the Netherlands. The night before my departure, a young man who often visited the guesthouse spoke to me. He said he admired the fact that I attended church, as very few of the tourists did so. He then told me about God as a father. I never remembered exactly what he said, but I knew what I felt.

…looking only at Jesus, the originator and perfecter of the faith, who for the joy set before Him endured the cross, despising the shame, and has sat down at the right hand of the throne of God.

—HEBREWS 12:2 (NASB)

A big load fell from my shoulders. *I don't have to do it alone anymore.* With that thought, all the little seeds that God had been planting in my heart over the past few months suddenly came into bloom. I realized that I had always processed events with my mind, but this was something I could feel with my heart—the knowledge that God was my Father, and He would accept me unconditionally. I had always felt out of place, as if people didn't truly like me, but none of that mattered now. I had the love of the Big Father. Peace filled me.

Keeping those things in my heart, I returned to Holland, leaving the unhappy version of myself in Ghana. The encounters God had brought my way had led me to surrender my life to Christ.

When I returned home, my atheist family and friends welcomed me, but not the fact that I had changed. They did not like the calm woman I had become. They labeled it as a "tropical sickness" that they believed I would eventually recover from. But when they saw I only got more on fire for Jesus and further engaged with the church, they branded me as brain-washed and were eager to "save" me. They even concocted a plan to abduct me. Eventually I was alienated from my family and lost all my friends.

Even though losing my loved ones wasn't easy, I held on to God's promises and remained steadfast in my choice, confident that it was the right one. God had orchestrated my trip to Ghana, from my extra funds to the divine encounters with all the people who, in their own unique way, planted a seed in my life. I was sure God would guide me through. He had found me while I wasn't looking for Him and brought me to a place where He could mold my heart. He transformed me from a touchy, independent woman to a fulfilled woman who depends on God.

In God's Hands
from the Start

Linda J. Reeves

My first clear memory, at three years old: walking in on a scene
of domestic violence. I fled to a hill behind our house and
stood there alone, shaking. In seconds, I felt something quickly
wrap around me, unseen but persistent. It pulled tighter until
it held my body still. In that moment of comfort, I knew three
things: my life would be painful, I'd never be alone, and I'd
always be safe.

I often stayed with my grandmother for weeks, even months,
at a time. She lived in the country and took me to church.
People there were friendly and talked a lot about God, and I
realized He was the presence that had surrounded me. I felt it
in their hugs at the end of the service and in the warm meals
my grandmother made with food from her garden. The fanci-
ful stories she told at bedtime helped me forget the turmoil at
home—until I started school.

My parents continued to fight, and my father sometimes
went away for long periods of time. He was gone the day I
heard my mother telling a friend, "Did you ever hear of getting a divorce on Valentine's Day?"

I ran to my brothers, who were older, and asked, "What's a
divorce?"

Shocked, they looked at each other and cried. I knew then Daddy would not be coming home.

But he did, once. It was late at night, and I heard his voice. Then a sound like a chair being knocked to the floor. I could hardly breathe until I heard footsteps coming down the hall. He slowly opened my bedroom door, and I closed my eyes. As we had often done, I pretended to be asleep so he could tease me, "Wake up!"

He stood quietly at the end of the bed while I waited. My foot was out of the covers, and he squeezed it. *Any time now,* I thought. Then he walked out, closing the door quickly behind him. I never saw my father again.

> ### And surely I am with you always, to the very end of the age.
>
> —MATTHEW 28:20 (NIV)

In that moment of sadness, as in others, I felt God's presence silently reminding me: *I know it's hard, but I'm here with you, and you are safe.*

Soon after, we moved into a small apartment. My mother worked long hours at a truck stop to support us. Despite her exhaustion, she often made us breakfast before school—cornmeal mush or biscuits. We liked the biscuits. My brothers and I worked at school for lunches and collected recyclables on weekends for extra money. I had just turned nine—proud to be half grown, as I saw it, and helping out.

Then one Sunday morning, Mama abruptly told us we needed to be in church. We didn't argue, because it meant going for a ride. She drove in our old car until she saw a steeple and pulled into the gravel lot across the street. We got out and lined up side by side, watching as people entered the building.

She hadn't been to church in a long time, and with five children in less than Sunday-perfect clothing, she hesitated.

One lady kept looking over her shoulder as she neared the open doors. Finally, she turned around, crossed the road, and motioned for us to come with her. She introduced herself as Mrs. Tortoris. She had a kind face and a soothing voice and wore a pretty white dress with bright blue flowers on it.

"I teach Sunday school," she told us. As we walked in, I had no idea this woman would set the course for the rest of my life.

When the service ended, she offered to pick us children up every week and take us back home after church. For Mother, it meant she could work on Sundays without worrying about where we were. So every week, we went—but it wasn't long until the boys stopped going, and then my younger sisters. I was the only one left who climbed eagerly into her car every Sunday.

She always checked in with Mama to make sure about spending time with me. One time I stayed at her house, and the first thing I saw was a shelf full of books in the living room. Pointing to them, I asked in wonder, "Are those yours?"

She laughed and said, "Yes, I keep a lot of books around for my nieces and nephews. You can read any of them you like."

I was afraid to touch them. Seeing my reluctance, she encouraged me to take a closer look. I sat on the floor in front of the shelf, lost in the titles and sensing I'd entered a new world. Mama had taken us to the library a few times, but I didn't think people could actually own books.

That evening we read a story together, something I'd never experienced, even at school. Feeling overwhelmed with happiness, I looked up at her and said, "You're different."

She laughed. "Oh?"

"You're nice all the time."

"You think so?"

I nodded. "What makes you like that?"

She thought about it, then smiled.

"I love Jesus, and I try to be like Him."

I knew who He was, but I needed more.

"Where is He?"

"In my heart," she said.

She could see I struggled to understand but quickly reassured me, "Just keep your heart open. He'll find you."

I didn't know how, but she seemed certain it would happen, and I didn't want to disappoint her. So I changed the subject.

"Why did you take us into church with you that day?"

She took a deep breath before speaking. "I saw your mother standing there with all you children, and it broke my heart. She looked so afraid, and I wanted her to know it was OK to come inside."

That was the first time, but not the last, that I told Mrs. Tortoris I loved her.

All too soon our family moved again—this time farther away. Our new house in a wooded area seemed isolated and unwelcoming. With Mother at work on weekends, we played too loudly and fought all the time. The noise! I wanted to find a church, a place of solace.

> **Then you will call, and the LORD will answer; you will cry for help, and he will say: Here am I.**
>
> **—ISAIAH 58:9 (NIV)**

One morning I left the house without telling anyone and started walking, not knowing exactly where I was going. I didn't realize it was Saturday and most churches wouldn't be open. I did, however, eventually see a parking lot filled with cars and a sign that read Vacation Bible School. I went in and sat down in the back.

Already nearing the end of his message, the preacher asked us to stand and sing a hymn. Words from the first verse had my attention: "Softly and tenderly Jesus is calling...waiting and watching...for you and for me." I fought tears when I heard the chorus: "Come home, come home. Ye who are weary, come home."

Briefly, I thought I saw someone standing by the preacher, looking right at me and holding out his arms. I blinked and the vision cleared. Suddenly, I understood! *He'll find you.* I ran down the aisle and took the preacher's hand.

"I want Jesus in my heart!" I said with certainty. He stared at me, nodding slowly but saying nothing. Gently, he guided me to a seat near the front. As he concluded the service, others gathered around me, shaking their heads and whispering.

One of the men sat down beside me and said, "My name's John. What's yours?"

As I answered, everyone else began asking questions.

"Are you here with someone? Where do you live? Where are your parents? Is there someone we can call to come get you? Have you been to any other church? Which one?"

Finally, I could help them! I remembered the name.

"Where is it?"

"I don't know."

"What's the preacher's name?"

"I'm not sure, but I know Mrs. Tortoris."

Jumping up, John announced, "I'll make some calls." He left the room and came back later, smiling.

"She's on her way!"

He told me she had to drive 45 miles to pick me up.

"She's really happy about the decision you made and can't wait to see you."

When she arrived, she hugged me and told me that because I'd decided that I wanted to invite Jesus into my heart, she'd make sure I was baptized. She shared that she'd also been baptized when she was nine. That made me feel even closer to her. Then she thanked everyone there for taking care of me, and we left.

On the way to the car, I confessed. "I don't know where I live."

"That's OK," she said. "I do."

As always, she delivered me safely home.

> I will say of the
> LORD, "He is my
> refuge and my
> fortress, my God,
> in whom I trust."
>
> —PSALM 91:2 (NIV)

The next day she helped me prepare for baptism in the church where we first met. After the ceremony, she gave me a white Bible with the inscription, *Always be the sweet girl you are now, dear, and the Lord will bless you.*

As a child, I didn't see Mrs. Tortoris again after the baptism. We lived too far away to visit, and we moved frequently as my mother looked for work. But as an adult, I discovered that she was living in a small country town and called the pastor of the church she was attending, wanting to surprise her with a visit.

It was a joyous reunion, and afterward, the pastor asked me to speak to the church about the ways Mrs. Tortoris had blessed my life. "Not too many people come back to say thank you," he explained.

I kept in touch with her by phone after that. I let her know that I've worked hard to live up to her expectations. I can't say I've been sweet all the time, but fortunately the Lord has blessed me anyway.

God found me when I was a lost and frightened child and held me tight to stop my trembling. From that day, I've trusted Him to help me face every adversity along the way. And He has kept His promise to stay with me and keep me safe, always.

Without Borders

Alejandro José Danilo Tabares

I don't remember the day I died inside. It seems so long ago.
I'm not altogether sure I was ever alive in the sense that I was
present in my own life.

My siblings and I grew up as a generation of pain. We watched
our father take the voices of our mother and grandmother with a
knife before we were old enough to be in school. Two mothers
died that day. Did we children die, too, on the inside? We
moved away, as far as the wind could take us, and lived with
other family members, but we never forgot the pain.

Addiction and depression followed me. I spent my late twenties
in and out of hospitals against my will. Family and friends called
to make wellness checks, and my home no longer felt safe. I
bounced around to different hotels throughout Manhattan, where
I was living at the time, and distanced myself from everyone.

My mental health continued to crumble. I researched how
to die and chose the least traumatic path. I collected my pre-
scriptions until I had enough to end my life and made final
preparations: phone upstairs and out of reach; me in the basement; milk to settle my stomach so it would accept the pills. I
remember surrendering to death as the pills took hold, but God
had other plans.

It may have been hours or days later when I came to. My
first thoughts were, *If I die here in the basement of this New York*

apartment, nobody will know why. They'll think I'm just another addict who overdosed. I did not want that to be my story!

When I fully awoke and had some time to think about what to do next, I decided to take a three-month medical leave. I left the country immediately with my dog, Lily, and headed for Puerto Rico. I still wanted to die, but a small part of me wondered if I might find peace and healing away from my high-pressure job in fashion design.

Eventually the call came: "It's time for you to come back to work."

Everything in me echoed silently, *I can't go back!* I had pursued every solution suggested and actively participated in every recovery program. Nothing worked. Death felt inevitable if I returned.

I contacted a charity and made plans to donate everything I owned in preparation for leaving the country indefinitely. I flew back to New York City to be there when their truck pulled up.

The next morning, Lily and I were on our way to the airport with a backpack, my meds, and her carrier bag. It was easy for me to let go of my old life. I still felt dead inside, and dead people don't own things. I often think of what my mom and grandmother may have left behind. Were their belongings thrown away, abandoned, and forgotten?

As the Uber drove, I decided where to go. Costa Rica came to mind. I had no plan other than to die in peace on a beach, and that seemed as good a place as any other, so I booked the next flight.

I consciously left everyone behind. There was no goodbye, no explanation. I even left myself—whatever I thought I was or could have been. I had a destination, but I had no idea what I was running from or to. I don't even remember the details of the flight. It seemed like I closed my eyes, and when I had the strength to open them again, I was on the beach and Lily was there helping me process the pain.

The ocean has many faces. Over the days that followed, I soaked in the calm, serene beauty. But below the surface, the riptides of my memories and emotions held quick and unexpected danger. When my heart dipped deep, there were jagged days of grief and torment. Other days fury swept in like a tropical storm. I was angry at people for not helping me, angry that they didn't know I needed help, angry at myself for not telling them.

Even so, more and more I found myself noticing how beautiful each day was, how perfect my surroundings were. And each day I thought, *It's too beautiful to die yet.*

> They hit me when I was down, but God stuck by me. He stood me up on a wide-open field; I stood there saved—surprised to be loved!
>
> —PSALM 18:18–19 (MSG)

I decided that I wanted to take myself off the antipsychotic meds before I died, so I would know I was thinking clearly. I went through withdrawals with my puppy in my arms. All I knew was to be still in the sand and listen to the ocean. Some days that's all I did. Lily sat with me, and I began to feel peace.

Somewhere in the stillness and listening, I heard God's voice again. I had always been a spiritual person. My grandfather was a pastor; I sang in the choir and played piano. Much of that had been silenced in my adult life, but gospel music remained a solace and inspiration.

One particular song revived hope: *Oceans*. I had first heard it at Hillsong Church in New York City, where I sometimes escaped to experience peace and song. Now it helped me become still as I sat by the water and grounded myself. I prayed. I sat in silence. I realized how tired I was from fighting just to "be."

I still expected to die, but I somehow knew I could trust God to provide for me until that day came. It was my first concrete form of hope, and from that hope, I woke up to my vibrant surroundings. The air was so fresh in Costa Rica! I rented a bicycle and began to ride everywhere with Lily in the basket. God allowed me to appreciate beauty again. I was finally in a good place.

When news of my brother's suicide reached me, God helped me keep moving. I did not go back to the US for my brother's funeral. I knew if I did, I would fall back into a state of depression and addiction. It was too soon. I stayed in Costa Rica to safely grieve from afar.

When I first got the news of my brother's death, I just drew the curtains and went to sleep—my go-to for any painful situation. When I woke, I remember lying there thinking, *I can't get out of bed.* But I also remembered my darkest days in New York, when I couldn't get up to do simple things like eat or drink. I thought, *If I don't get out of bed, I may as well be in New York.* I urged myself repeatedly, *You've got to get out of bed!*

I forced myself to take Lily to the beach. Before long, I started singing. Then the thought came: *I just need to play piano and sing.*

I got up and looked for a church with a piano in the little town. It was the week between Christmas and New Year's Eve, and they were all closed. I finally found a man and his son cleaning at one. They didn't have a piano, but they had an organ.

He turned out to be the pastor and brought his whole family in to watch while I sang and cried and tried to figure out how to play the organ. I was so surrendered that I didn't care about having an audience. I grieved for my brother. I grieved for all the people I loved who died. I even went through the motions of grief for myself. When I was done, I felt like it was OK to move on.

In the days that followed, I cut grief loose and withdrew my hand from torment. I embraced worship and imagined bringing those I loved with me as I moved forward into life again. Through it all, the lyrics to the song "Oceans" stayed with me:

You call me out upon the waters
The great unknown where feet may fail
And there I find You in the mystery
In oceans deep my faith will stand…
Spirit lead me where my trust is without borders★

That worship song held me tightly as I left Costa Rica, the place of my grieving. I moved on, trusting God anew, to Nicaragua. The hostels there were shared dormitories with loud parties. After only one night, I knew I could not handle that scene and walked around until I found a quiet place: Sin Fronteras. I didn't know Spanish, or what its name meant.

After I'd been there a while, I noticed the place needed some updates. The business systems, the hotel design and facilities, the marketing—all of it needed a refresh, and that was something I

★"Oceans (Where Feet May Fail)," © 2013 Capitol CMG Publishing, written by Joel Houston, Matt Crocker, and Salomon Lighthelm.

GOD'S GIFT OF HEARING
— Buck Storm —

A SHEPHERD SINGS. His voice echoes through canyons and bounces off crags. The sheep come because they know who they belong to, who loves and cares for them. Other voices might be ignored, *should* be ignored, but the voice of the shepherd is always obeyed. Because the shepherd is love.

My own Shepherd sings, His voice echoing through galaxies and bouncing off stars. It is a miracle He calls me at all. And continues to call me even when I wander.

Listen for His voice. He sings. And His song is the most beautiful sound we can ever hear.

---

could do. Little did I know that it would start a new life path of helping businesses redesign and renovate.

One day, after hearing me play "Oceans" on repeat, the owner asked me to look up the lyrics in Spanish. The song came up with a different title: "Sin Fronteras"! By matching the lyrics, I understood that it meant "without borders." It was the perfect intersection of the song that lifted me out of my old life and the place God led me to where my new life began.

Redesigning Sin Fronteras marked my resurrection into a new direction of helping others. I had surrendered to death more than once in my personal journey, but when I surrendered to trusting God, I came to life.

Prayer and Penicillin

Marcella Rejoice Ruch

Colorful swear words turned the waiting room air blue the first night our clinic opened. The patient, Beth, had been bleeding for ten years, and years of pain had fueled her fierce anger—anger at God, at doctors, at hospitals, and at the world. She reminded me of the woman who touched the hem of Jesus's garment. After Jesus felt power go out of Him, He turned to her and told her that her faith had healed her (Matthew 9:22).

Beth had been rejected from many health facilities because she lacked health insurance. Intimidated by her shouting, but firmly committed to Christ's ideal of service, the staff welcomed and reassured her. After her free surgery, she regained a healthy, vibrant body. Slowly Beth healed from the depression, sadness, and deep bitterness that had sunk into her body, mind, and soul. It took years of loving care. Like the woman who touched the hem of His garment, a different kind of power healed Beth: the power of Christian love in action.

★★★

A year earlier, while at a conference on evangelism, God grabbed me by the collar, sat me up in my seat, and made me give Him hyper-attention. He lay a command on my two shoulders: *Go home! Open a free clinic for the poor in Colorado Springs.*

Wow! A powerful call from God to do a new thing at sixty-three years old. I had no medical background. My educational career had little prepared me for creating a medical clinic. Why me? Yet the call was real. Goose bumps covered my whole body.

As I pondered the bombshell instruction to open a free clinic, I realized God wanted a place where prayer and penicillin would be available in the same location. I prayed daily about each next step, and at every step along the way, God provided.

> But Jesus turned around, and when He saw her He said, "Be of good cheer, daughter; your faith has made you well."
>
> —MATTHEW 9:22 (NKJV)

The public library agreed to let me use a meeting room. An article in the local newspaper announced the start of a new free clinic for the poor. People from all walks of life attended the gathering: doctors and nurses, plus nonmedical people like receptionists and maintenance people who believed in the idea and wanted to help. This was the first group of volunteers.

My pastor gave me his blessing and advised me to form a legal nonprofit organization. He also allowed me to hold a monthly meeting at the church and put an announcement in the church bulletin. Lots of church members with medical backgrounds showed up and offered their skills. One nurse brought along her husband, who announced that he knew nothing about medicine since he was a financial officer. He became our treasurer.

The local legal association provided a pro bono lawyer to advise us on nonprofit incorporation. He told us to form a board of directors. I took the need to my weekly ecumenical prayer group, and that very day they decided they would become the board of directors. They agreed immediately on who would be the president, vice president, treasurer, and secretary. A few other members offered to be directors, since we needed twelve board members. The lawyer filed names and addresses with the secretary of state, and Mission Medical Clinic (MMC) became a legal entity.

> **Ask, and it will be given to you; seek, and you will find; knock, and it will be opened to you.**
>
> **—MATTHEW 7:7 (NKJV)**

God sent us a retired MD to be medical director. Later, he shared with me that the volunteer work for Mission Medical Clinic had saved his life while he was healing from serious depression after the loss of his wife.

In my own church, a pharmacist volunteered to oversee all medications. He compiled an affordable formulary with the medications to treat nearly every sickness. In the beginning he carried the meds to the clinic in a suitcase and took them safely home again once the clinic closed. Only after we had our own building did he organize a full dispensary. He and his wife began a pharmacy assistance program to help our patients file the paperwork to get free medications from pharmaceutical companies.

Our executive director organized the volunteers into a staff, and the clinic was born.

The local pregnancy center offered to share space with us on Thursday evening and Saturday morning, when they were closed. During our first year, those became our regular hours. Patients poured in for our free services, and it soon became clear that we needed our own space. Prayer time, big-time!

While attending a reception for a large medical organization, I noticed I was standing by the CEO of the local city hospital. I asked God, "Is there a reason I am here and he is here next to me?"

God answered, *Yes!*

The local hospitals had been giving MMC free labs and X-rays for all of our patients. I turned to this tall, kindly administrator, introduced myself, and thanked him for the free services. Then I quickly added, "Did you know that we must move again? I'm wondering if you might have an empty clinic building somewhere in the city that we might use?"

Thoughtfully, he answered, "Possibly. I'll ask around."

He was true to his word and found us a thirty-thousand-square-foot building, vacant a long time, in need of lots of love. We leased it for a dollar a year. They offered to pay all utilities, and our volunteers painted, repaired, and created a beautiful, clean, professional site for ongoing operations. Furniture and medical equipment poured in to furnish three fully outfitted clinic exam rooms, a prayer room, offices, and a gorgeous waiting room. We opened using less than a quarter of the space. Soon, because God sent a volunteer endocrinologist, we expanded to add an additional diabetic clinic as large as our primary care clinic. Later we would expand again to turn part of the lower level into a four-bay dental clinic and an eye ministry that included an optometrist, an ophthalmologist, and free glasses for anyone in need.

In a few years, MMC had two hundred volunteers, helped thousands of patients, and was open for clinical services every day except Sunday. We had support from about one hundred churches. It was a miracle in action.

Then the city council voted to sell our building. The asking price of nearly a million dollars was overwhelming to our board of directors, but after I offered to chair our fundraising efforts, the board agreed to go ahead with efforts to raise the money needed to buy the building.

God saw our need and heard our prayers. The hospital gave us a contract to purchase that contained a marvelous surprise: The purchase price would be $960,000, but the hospital was offering MMC a $360,000 credit for outstanding community service. That meant we only had to raise $600,000.

> **Then Jesus went about all the cities and villages, teaching in their synagogues, preaching the gospel of the kingdom, and healing every sickness and every disease among the people.**
>
> —MATTHEW 9:35 (NKJV)

Every one of our two hundred volunteers seemed to help. Dollars poured in from churches, from volunteers who dug deep and found a few thousand dollars, and even patients gave money. A single very generous donor gave $120,000. With the gifts from him and the larger community, we purchased the building.

When I retired from MMC, the party was really a celebration of the volunteers who had made so much possible. Everybody came. I was at a loss for words. The room was full of love and joy.

The cheering went on and on. They were cheering for God, for the plan He gave me, for themselves, for all the hard work, for the new friends made, for the thousands of patients helped, for the millions of dollars of medication given at no charge. They were rejoicing at being a part of His Kingdom while they were alive on this earth. What a happy time.

Now, Mission Medical serves as a site for the Anschutz Medical School in Denver, Colorado, to help train future doctors. COVID-19 nearly killed the clinic, but it is slowly regaining its ability to be a gift to the community, especially to all the migrants from other countries not able to access expanded Medicare. God is still using MMC. Years ago He gave me a command but also blessed me in so many ways to make it happen. With His love and constant support, we continue to heal the sick in the name of Jesus.

To one who has faith, no explanation is necessary. To one without faith, no explanation is possible.

—Thomas Aquinas

CHAPTER 7

Miracle Moments

Every Church
Is a Small Town

Allison Lynn

Leading worship at the front of the church gives a good knowledge of your congregation. You learn who likes to move around
the sanctuary and who claims the same pew every week. You
see friendships grow as people sit side by side, and disputes
brewing as couples start to sit a little farther apart. You see who
comes in late, who loves to sing, and who takes that little nap
during the sermon.

As worship leaders, my husband, Gerald, and I treasured
this opportunity to learn about our community through this
unique perspective. Our congregation was a conservative group.
They had been raised on "proper" church behavior—dress well,
arrive on time, greet your neighbor, follow the service, and
when it was all done, go out into the hall for coffee hour. Our
people weren't given to hands in the air, spontaneous prayers, or
outbursts of public emotion. Most Sunday mornings passed in a
predictable, stoic way.

But one Sunday, from our front-stage view, we witnessed
something that forever changed our reserved gatherings.

It was a week after Easter and the sanctuary was still filled
with the scent of lilies and the echoes of "He is Risen!" People
entered the church still feeling the joy of the season. Some

families had taken holidays, as evidenced by suntans and relaxed smiles. As each person found their regular pew, they gently nodded to their neighbors and offered subtle waves of greeting.

As it got closer to the start of worship, our minister pulled us aside. "We had some terrible news yesterday. I'm going to share it with the congregation. I'm sure people will be upset, but after I make the announcement, we'll just carry on with the service as planned."

Gerald and I took our positions with the band and watched as the minister stepped up to the microphone.

"Friends, I received an upsetting phone call last night. You all know the Martins' son…" Our minister started to unfold the

> ## For where two or three gather in my name, there am I with them.
>
> —MATTHEW 18:20 (NIV)

difficult story of a healthy young man—a husband and a father of three young children—who went for a run in the beautiful spring weather, only to come home clutching his chest. An undiagnosed heart defect caused a heart attack. He didn't stand a chance. He passed away within minutes.

All eyes turned to the Martins. They were in their regular front row pew, but today, they were sitting closer than usual, their arms linked together. This stalwart couple of the church, leaders of our community, and strong vibrant people were suddenly facing the greatest tragedy of their lives.

As our minister shared the heartbreaking news, there were gasps of shock. No one could believe what they were hearing. But then, something unexpected started to happen within the congregation. What appeared to be a wave pulsed through the crowd.

Our traditionally staid congregation was starting to move. Without prompting or invitation, they were leaving their pews and coming toward the Martins. Hands were laid on their shoulders. People leaned over one another to hug and touch the grieving couple. Words of compassion were whispered in intimate companionship.

Gerald and I couldn't believe what we were witnessing. Our reserved community was breaking all the customs of church decorum. The rules of etiquette were dissolving in the face of such a tragedy. As the dam broke, the floodwaters of compassion could not be stopped.

> **Rejoice with those who rejoice; mourn with those who mourn.**
>
> —ROMANS 12:15 (NIV)

As we saw the swirling of love around this grieving couple, Gerald started to play some gentle guitar music. Something holy was happening. In its own way, this was a moment of worship, offering the best of our hearts to someone in need, extending God's love in an expression of compassion. We were mourning with those who mourned, and joining in God's mission to heal the brokenhearted.

As hugs were given and condolences whispered, the wave gradually calmed. The congregation seemed to take a collective breath. Slowly, people returned to their pews. They wiped their eyes and regained their composure. They took deep breaths and prepared themselves for worship, not realizing the worship had already begun.

We started the opening hymn, and the voices soared to the rafters! Our Easter songs sang of resurrection, God's promises fulfilled, and life conquering death. Without having to say it, we all felt the desperate need for those truths to be real. More than ever, we needed to know that life wins, heaven is real, and God is ever-present in our time of need.

As Gerald and I made our way home that afternoon, we couldn't help but talk about what we had just witnessed. Gerald said, "You know, it was like, for just a few minutes, our big-city church became a small town."

Within a few days, I started to hear a new song drifting through the house. Gerald came to me with a lyric and a melody. "I could use some harmonies on this..."

In front of me was the story of our church. It began:

When the Martins' son passed away.
Everybody there on that Sunday,
Gave every bit of strength they had to them.

When Monique and Jason got married,
Their invite was the blessing that week,
It said, "If you've got good wishes, bring 'em."

The pews are just like a front porch swing.
Man I'm telling you, you should hear us sing!

Every church is a small town,
It doesn't matter where you're found.
Something about that hallowed ground
And the deep down Gospel sound.
Every church is a small town★

★Lyrics from "Every Church Is a Small Town." Written by Gerald Flemming. SOCAN © 2012. Used with permission.

GOD'S GIFT OF HEARING
— Heidi Gaul —

IF YOU'RE LIKE me, hearing a few lines of a nursery song can instantly transport you back to your childhood. For some of us, memories might be triggered by the *clack-clack* of a train rushing past on the tracks, or the *clop-clop* of horses' hooves on a dusty lane.

The sounds we hear are more than noise. They encapsulate our past experiences and help us maneuver through the present. God guides and comforts us through the miracle of hearing. Can I hear an "Amen!"?

After that Sunday morning, people still wore their Sunday best, arrived on time, and followed the traditional rules of church etiquette, but something had shifted.

Morning greetings changed from polite waves to generous hugs. Honest conversations about grief and spiritual challenges became the norm. And it no longer seemed unusual when someone got up during the service to go sit with someone who was obviously struggling. The walls of "proper church behavior" had fallen, and we were so much better for it.

Gerald and I eventually left that church to start a traveling ministry. Since that time, we've sung "Every Church Is a Small Town" across Canada and the United States. We've sung it in city churches, rural churches, big churches, little churches, and churches that aren't even in churches. We tell the story of the miraculous, God-inspired moment that sparked the song. And without fail, someone will come up to us and say, "You know, you could have written that about us! That's exactly what our church is like too."

And we always smile because it's always true. In our best moments, the church is a community unlike any other. We hold the hands of the grieving, and we pray over new marriages. We welcome strangers, prodigals, seekers, and stragglers. We embrace seniors with a lifetime of faithfulness and teenagers with rebellious questions. We feed one another, laugh with one another, and lift our voices in praise-filled harmony. Whether one of us suffers or celebrates, we all feel it and we're all in it together.

In the best kind of way, every church really is a small town.

God Is an Eleventh-Hour God

Laurie Davies

The explosive smell of the airbag put me in a state of urgency. I thought I was spinning. A swirl of fall colors and horizon told me I must be spinning.

I had just crested the last hill before home driving 65 miles an hour. I remember seeing an oncoming car turn into my lane. Like a child gripping a Tilt-A-Whirl's lap bar, I clutched the steering wheel and braced for impact.

The rest is a crystal-clear blur. A blur because I spun two or maybe three 360-degree circles in just seconds. Crystal clear because I had three distinct, prolonged thoughts in that very short span. God was the only one I wanted to talk to in that muffled, in-between moment between death and life. I knew He was right there.

God, will Greg be OK without me? Please God, take care of him. He'll be lonely in our big country house. Let him find a wife quickly. Let him know I'd want that. Please let her be funny and pretty and willing to help him carry the pressures he feels in this life.

Greg and I had been married only four years, but it was long enough for me to know he didn't like being alone.

I spun and sensed in a powerful way that Greg would be just fine.

But, God, I never got to be a mom! Greg and I had always talked about having four kids. I wonder if we would have had any boys. Greg really wanted a bunch of boys. Why did we wait? I'm so glad we waited.

I knew in that moment that Greg would be a dad.

And what about my column? Why didn't I file it before I left? Why am I thinking about work? They'll probably write, "She didn't have time to die—she was on deadline," on my tombstone. I worked hard on that column, though. I don't think my editor knows where it is on the server . . .

And just like that, the Tilt-A-Whirl stopped. My SUV rocked slightly onto both left tires before the right side slammed hard onto the pavement of the two-lane Texas highway. My car alarm blared, though there was no one in the remote area to hear it besides me and the other driver.

> You will be secure, because there is hope; you will look about you and take your rest in safety. You will lie down, with no one to make you afraid.
>
> — JOB 11:18–19 (NIV)

The blistering smell of the airbag now blending with burned rubber from my tires, I instinctively reached for the door handle and scampered out of the driver's seat. I walked over to the shoulder of the highway and sat down onto the rocks, relieved. I was OK. A quick check told me the guy in the other car was OK too.

I wouldn't see until later that the front of my SUV crumpled like an accordion until it stopped cold at the passenger cab—as if a wall of angels had set a boundary.

I called 911 and my husband. This was a back stretch of highway. It would be a while before anyone arrived.

***

A few years later, my grandpa was on his deathbed. I'd made many trips to see him when he was living. But he went downhill quickly, and I couldn't get to him now that he was dying. He was only able to draw breaths in short, frequent gasps. I called my grandma.

"He can't speak, honey. The best I can do is hold the phone up to his ear."

"OK," I agreed weakly.

I fumbled through words and tears, not knowing if he could even hear me. Grandma said he could still hold small pieces of paper. This gave me an idea.

I scrawled out a short note. Blurred in a few spots by tears, I figured my grandpa could still read it. He'd always been good at reading me. When I lost my Raggedy Ann doll, he settled my hysteria. The year I got braces and a bad perm, he somehow convinced me I was beautiful. After college when I sobbed because I couldn't find a job, he said that obviously no one with an eye for talent had interviewed me yet.

In all the times we'd walked and talked—me slowing our pace when I was a girl by balancing on every front-yard retaining wall like it was a tightrope—we'd never talked about faith. His generation didn't do that much. The most important words had been left unsaid.

Dear Grandpa: You've been the closest picture of God's love to me on earth. Jesus loves you and I wish we would have talked about it. I think the retaining walls in heaven are made of gold and I want to hold your hand while I balance on them. You'll be there, right? It's as simple as John 3:16. Ask Grandma to read that to you. I love you. —L

I overnighted my note, swallowing hard knowing the $30 overnight fee would mean a cut to the grocery budget that week.

He never got the note.

He died hours before it arrived.

God, couldn't You have kept him alive long enough?

I couldn't make sense of it. Grief. Anger. Confusion. Longing. The finality of it all took my breath away. So, I did what I'd done a thousand other times to make sense of the world. I put my pen to the page of a journal. Unbelievably my writing prompt for that day was: Ask God what He wants to say to you today.

Still smarting, I asked Him.

> The Lord is not slow in keeping his promise, as some understand slowness. Instead he is patient with you, not wanting anyone to perish, but everyone to come to repentance.
>
> —2 PETER 3:9 (NIV)

These words immediately came: *My child, don't you remember what I taught you in Texas? I was as close to your grandpa as I was to you in that spinning car. I'm an eleventh-hour God.*

★★★

"Ma'am, can you hear me? Are you OK?"

I stood up from the Texas roadside. Sea legs betrayed me and I sat quickly back down. I looked up at the state trooper. Sunlight silhouetted his entire frame. From my view on the ground, he looked like a twenty-foot-tall angel.

"You were pretty fortunate out here today, ma'am. People don't usually walk away from a crash like this one," he said.

"When they do," I asked slowly, my ears ringing, "do they say their thoughts sped up or time slowed down?"

"All the time." He nodded.

"Because I had three really long thoughts and I think it was God showing me that He can do anything—*anything*—in the final seconds of a life. He can allow people to believe in Him quickly. He can fix things in seconds. My notepad is in my purse. I've got to write this down."

I tried again to get to my feet, but I was still woozy. The trooper half-smiled and gestured for me to stay put.

"We'll get your purse. Is your registration in your vehicle?" he asked.

"Yes, but that's not what is important—"

"Is it OK with you if I get your purse?" he persisted.

"Yes, but—"

The trooper stepped closer to me. His wide-brimmed khaki hat cast a late-day shadow on me.

"But," he said, "God is an eleventh-hour God."

"Are you a—"

"Christian," he interrupted. "Yes."

I let him finish his report. My husband arrived and took me to the hospital. Remarkably, initial tests didn't show a need for anything but ice and ibuprofen. I'd probably have some pain from whiplash. The minor burns on my chest from the airbag would heal.

"God is an eleventh-hour God." I kept repeating the trooper's words over and over.

Looking back, I think my grandpa already knew where he stood with God. My grandma—in her stoic German and generational fashion—later told me that she read my FedExed letter and she was sure my grandpa "would have agreed."

The bigger picture was the glimpse God gave me into His ways. I discovered that God can do anything He wants when it counts. He can slow down time. He can speed up the mind's ability to think clearly. Neurophysiologists credit this common "time standing still" phenomenon to the "blue spot" deep in the brain that dumps epinephrine into the body to help hyper-focus our attention.

But I credit the God who wired it all. He opens His heaven to workers who show up late just the same as He opens it to those who show up early. He knew some would show up late. He can work in as much time as He needs to, be it a fraction of a second—or the eleventh hour.

In His grace, He made a way.

Hearing God in the Desert

B. Anne Stevens

One of my happiest moments was in October 1998, when my husband, Steve, was appointed to his first pastorate at a small country church in Riverside County, California. "We believe you are the right family for this appointment," said the district director. Elated, we moved into the parsonage, located next door to an elementary school. Perfect for a stay-at-home mom of four young sons. I embraced my new role as a pastor's wife. Life was good. Never once did I think, *What if this doesn't work out?*

In May 2001, one of my worst moments happened when we were again called to meet with the district director. We were blindsided. "The elementary school purchased the land, and we are closing the church. You have thirty days to move out of the parsonage." The room blurred and the words were distant as he talked. Incomprehensible. Why would God move us here only to take us away?

We began the quest for housing, but because our income had been limited to my husband's side hustle and part-time ministry pay, we had no savings. Our search for a place we could afford was futile. To add to our injury, the company Steve worked for part-time dissolved his position. All income stopped. Shortly after, Steve was offered a staff position at a large church in downtown Riverside, but it didn't start for two months. With less than a week before the thirty-day deadline, we were offered a place to stay with extended family in Phelan, north of the San Gabriel mountains, in the Mojave Desert.

We placed most of our belongings in storage and moved an hour from Riverside into half of a large ranch-style home, miles from civilization. We crammed into two bedrooms and a bathroom. I tried to be strong while arranging our necessities, but I broke down while unpacking bath products into someone else's shower. I was defeated. Heartbroken. Thirty days prior, I had a home, a ministry, and a purpose. Now we were home-less. No church. No job. What purpose was this? To top it off, we were in the middle of an actual desert.

> I will take you as my own people, and I will be your God.
>
> —EXODUS 6:7 (NIV)

The view in every direction featured Joshua trees, yucca, cacti, and tumbleweeds. Neighbors were dozens of acres apart, intruders in the habitat for scorpions and packs of wild dogs. Sporadic dust devils mocked us. Monster insects invaded personal space. How could anyone live out here? How did this happen? We had been serving Jesus. It didn't make sense.

"We'll only be here one month," I assured our hosts. "Just until we find a rental in Riverside." I hated being dependent on another family. Steve made himself busy with side jobs until his new position started, but any income was sparse.

"Do your kids really drink that much milk?" The question tore through me like a bullet as I realized my in-laws felt the burden of our four children, in addition to their three. Our pitiful contributions were not enough. We needed money and a house, but with no current income, our prospects weren't good. Stress mounted to unbearable levels as we sent off countless rental applications.

Seeking alone time to think, I braved the desert and walked the dirt roads around our in-law's property. Resentment shrouded the natural beauty around me. Under other circumstances I might have enjoyed watching jackrabbits, but I was hurt, humiliated, and confused. Prayer was my only outlet. I wasn't quiet.

"God, what did I do wrong?" I fell to my knees. "I thought we were doing Your work. Why are we here?" I pleaded for rescue. "We can't even help with groceries."

Three weeks into our plight, something incredible happened. A pickup truck arrived followed by a cargo van, both full of boxes of food. Men got out and unloaded. A little Phelan church had heard about the stranded pastor's family and took a collection for the eleven people in one house. The boxes kept coming. It was no small donation. Food in bulk, meats, breads, pastas, and more. Even toilet paper!

A kind woman walked to where I stood with my jaw on the ground. "This is because God sees you." The woman hugged me.

"I don't know what to do," I said, tears brimming.

"You don't have to do anything," she said. "Trust God to take care of it."

It took all afternoon to make room in various cabinets. We had brought a deep freezer when we moved, and we packed it to the top with meat. Afterward, the two families prayed together to thank the Lord for His provision.

That night I went for a walk under the bright, twinkling stars. With no air pollution or streetlights, the hazy Milky Way glow illuminated the paths enough to see any coiled snakes. The most beautiful sky I'd ever seen. I was overwhelmed. "God, what just happened?"

The story of the Israelites came to mind. I could relate! When they cried for food, God brought them manna and quail. God sent us manna. And thankfully, we had better options than the quail that ran around the brush. Intrigued, I turned to Scripture to study the journey of Israel in the wilderness.

One month turned into two. Steve's employment started at the new church, but it would take a while to make up overdue bills and prepare for moving expenses. He traveled back and forth in our one vehicle every day, leaving early and coming back late. I tried to make the best of things, but we had already been in the desert twice as long as we'd expected, and there

> **My sheep listen to my voice; I know them, and they follow me.**
>
> —JOHN 10:27 (NIV)

was no end in sight. Helpless, there was only one thing I could do: Surrender. Everything. My hopes and dreams. My identity as a pastor's wife. Even my children, husband, and my home. Everything belonged to God. I had to trust Him.

Two months turned into three. There were more miracles. I found bunk beds for the boys at a yard sale for the exact amount of cash we had on hand. Someone gave me five pairs of shoes in just my size. A church couple gave us a car, giving us more flexibility to get around.

Every night I walked in the desert to breathe the fresh air and pray. I'd always found God in nature. Those walks were my lifeline. Inspired by the story of the Israelites, I began a deeper study of Exodus. The Israelites had a lot of setbacks due to disobedience. God led them to the Promised Land, but they took a forty-year detour because they didn't listen.

"Lord, please don't let this take forty years." Many moonlit hours were spent sitting on a rock or in the dirt. I prayed and worshipped under the same galaxy that blanketed the Israelites so long ago.

> So do not worry, saying, "What shall we eat?" or ... "What shall we wear?" For ... your heavenly Father knows that you need them.
>
> —MATTHEW 6:31–32 (NIV)

Breakthrough began in my heart as I sought God's will. I asked for forgiveness. I had set up my own kingdom with expectations of a perfect ministry life. I came to understand that God was not trying to take my life away; He wanted to give me so much more.

My prayers shifted. I stopped saying, "Get me out of here," and instead, "What do You want me to learn from this?" The desire to hear God's voice took over, and He met me there. Just like God provided the Israelites with water from a rock, His sweet presence washed over me.

At the end of four months, we were elated as we packed to move into our new home in Riverside. I went to the garage to clean out the freezer. I opened the lid and stopped. A single ham rested at the bottom. We did not buy meat that whole time. Stunned, I went inside. A few canned goods and staple items remained in the cabinets. Except for perishables, we had not bought groceries for over three months. Holding back

GOD'S GIFT OF TASTE
— Buck Storm —

I SAW THE sign on a Jerusalem back street—"World's Greatest Falafel"

Hmm, be careful, pal. I've had falafel everywhere from Los Angeles to Cairo. I stepped up to the counter. "Really? In the world?"

He shrugged. "You don't think so, you don't pay."

I tasted the falafel. "OK, you win." I pulled out my shekels.

"Taste and see that the LORD is good" (Psalm 34:8, NIV).

I guess I've questioned that one at times too. Then I taste and wonder, for the life of me, why I waited so long.

God wins. And He doesn't even want shekels.

---

tears, I went to clean the bathroom. As I pulled the bottles of shampoo and bath products from the shower, they felt empty. I shook them. Nothing. Realization flooded me. These were the exact bottles of soap I brought with us four months prior, and we had not bought new ones. Yesterday they were full enough, but today they were empty. With all the stress, soap was the last thing on my mind. But God took care of all our needs. Even soap.

The backyard of our new home had ten fruit trees, including citrus, figs, pomegranates, and plums. The foliage-rich neighborhood made for great prayer walks. A little hill behind the neighborhood had a wonderful rock for me to sit and survey our own promised land. God's grace through our wilderness changed me in many ways, including my approach to ministry, my priorities, and my relationships with others. My walk with Jesus was closer than ever, and I wouldn't trade that for anything. I am forever thankful for the time God led us through the desert, the place where I learned to hear His voice.

I Looked into the Eyes of God

Amanda Pennock

As I held my newborn granddaughter in my arms for the first time and looked into her eyes, I saw God looking back at me. It was at that moment that I knew I needed to change my life.

It was a hot summer morning in June 2015. My husband and I were packing our car for a long trip to see our grand-daughter for the first time. It was almost time to leave. There was just one more item to pack: my cooler of alcohol. I couldn't imagine taking such a long trip without that.

How did I get to this point where I depended so much on alcohol to make it through my day? Just a few years earlier I was a preschool teacher and a leader in my church. I had been a youth group leader, taught Bible studies at my home, and went on mission trips. Life had been so good! I was the happiest I had ever been in my life. I had it all, my husband had a success-ful business, I had a great marriage, friends, a nice house, nice cars, even a yacht in St. Martin. Then, after ten years at church, we decided to leave after some disagreements with the way the church was heading.

Soon after leaving the church, things started going downhill. The business started struggling, the yacht was lost in a hurri-cane, and our marriage was falling apart. I started drinking.

I quit reading my Bible and praying. I had become very depressed and had to start going to a counselor.

***

I was brought up with an abusive, alcoholic father. Growing up, I lived in constant fear for my life. I remember one night when my dad was drunk and got his gun out. He put one bullet in it and put the gun to his head, pulling the trigger. He thought it was a funny game. My mom grabbed his legs, begging him to stop as he was dragging her down the hallway. On another occasion, I woke up in my bed to discover a bullet hole in my wall. My dad's gun had gone off and the bullet had gone through my bedroom wall. I was around eight years old.

> **Children are a heritage from the LORD, offspring a reward from Him.**
>
> —PSALM 127:3 (NIV)

For years I searched for happiness. I had been in and out of bouts of drinking and getting high, but nothing helped fill the void inside me. At the age of fourteen, I even attempted suicide. I did manage to graduate from high school and was married and expecting my first child within three months of graduation.

In the first few years of marriage, I continued to use drugs and alcohol to help me cope with life. My husband was in the military and was gone a lot, leaving me alone to take care of the children and household. Every time I was involved in church, I would not feel the need to drink or do drugs. If I put God first in my life and put my faith in Him, I didn't feel the pressure of having to do everything myself, because I let God be in control.

But every time we relocated and got out of church, I would start back drinking and doing drugs.

***

This time, I had been drinking for about 8 years when my first granddaughter was born. I hated the person who I saw in the mirror, but felt like I had no hope of ever getting better. I even brought my daughter some alcohol to celebrate her becoming a mother.

Then it happened—the moment that my life would be changed forever. It was the moment that I saw God through the eyes of my newborn granddaughter. I can't describe the feeling. I had felt it before. It had been a long time, but I knew it was God's Holy Spirit coming over me. He reminded me how much He loves me and how He gives me a hope and a future. I felt complete love and a presence I had not felt in such a long time. I knew I had to make a change, if not for me, then for that tiny little girl I was holding in my arms.

> **Children's children are a crown to the aged, and parents are the pride of their children.**
>
> **—PROVERBS 17:6 (NIV)**

I didn't tell anyone about what I'd experienced, and I continued drinking for the next couple of weeks. Then, on the Fourth of July 2015, I took my last drink. I had gotten drunk and was driving, and my friend told me I was going to kill myself or someone else. It was that night, lying on the floor of my bedroom closet, that I cried out to God for help. I surrendered all to Him. He was there for me, like He always was.

My counselor recommended that I find an Alcoholics Anonymous meeting to get the help I needed to stop drinking. I didn't think I was an alcoholic because I compared myself to my dad. But I found out that the only requirement for membership is a desire to stop drinking, and that's what I had.

As I went to meetings, I listened to others share their stories, and it gave me hope. Someone helped me through the 12-step program, and I got back into church. I started reading the Bible again and praying. I started helping others and getting involved. My life had new meaning! I had a purpose! After just a little over a year being sober, I was invited to share my story with an auditorium full of military men and women who were graduating from a substance-abuse program.

> **For your Maker is your husband, the LORD of hosts is his name; and the Holy One of Israel is your Redeemer, the God of the whole earth he is called.**
>
> —ISAIAH 54:5 (ESV)

That first year wasn't easy. My marriage ended after almost 40 years. I had all new friends and had bought my first condo. I found myself, at 56 years old, alone for the first time in my life. It was during that time that I grew closer to God than I have ever been. He was my Creator, my best friend, and my husband.

After my divorce was final, my daughter invited me to move to be closer to her and her two daughters—the second girl having been born three years after the first. I sold my condo and moved thousands of miles away from my home state of

26 years. It was a very hard time, but God, my family, and my new friends were there for me. I immediately found AA meetings to attend and started going to church.

Just the other day my daughter had told me that my granddaughter was bragging about her grandma to her friends at the bus stop. I am blessed to be a part of her and her sister's life. If I had not gotten help, I never would have been able to be there for them. My granddaughter just celebrated her eighth birthday, and I just celebrated eight years of sobriety.

I am living a life that I never could have imagined. I am now remarried and travel all over the world bringing hope to others. One of the things I was told during my recovery was, "Don't give up before the miracle happens." I have found this to be so true. In times when I felt like giving up, I would remember this phrase and hold on to that promise. And when I did, the miracle always happened!

Divinely Remembered

Terri J. Kirby

As I stepped through the sliding doors into the nursing home, the air was thick with an unmistakable antiseptic aroma. I was greeted by shrill door alarms, the rhythmic tones of medical equipment, and other sounds common to an institutional setting. My senses were assaulted as I headed down the hall to locate my dad for my first visit since his admittance to the home.

And then I found him. Once a pillar of strength, Dad was now a frail figure, barely moving his bony legs as he shuffled slowly down the hall. His body was now in a constant state of restlessness and deterioration. His eyes, clouded by the haze of Alzheimer's, stared into the abyss of forgotten memories.

I followed him as he meandered to the lobby. Seeing Dad outside his room evoked a feeling of appreciation for the patience of the staff allowing him to wander within the safety of the locked doors. As I drew closer to him, childhood memories rushed over me.

★★★

Born with dwarfism, I was once a tiny bundle in my father's arms. He carried me not just as an infant but as a young child whose legs tired more easily than those of her other family members. On countless occasions he sat with me when fatigue overcame my limbs during family shopping expeditions. I have such fond memories of sipping an iced soda and munching salty french fries at our mall's Sweet William Restaurant while my mom and sister shopped.

Throughout my childhood, he fostered my independence in spite of my physical limitations. Although I was merely three feet tall, he encouraged me to follow my dreams and stretch past my comfort zone in a world not built to my size. For example, in elementary school he arranged for me to be an acolyte at our church services. I could not raise the snuffer high enough over the tall candles to put out the flames, so I was always paired with my average-sized sister. I would light the candles at the start of the service, and she would extinguish them at the end.

> In the same way, the Spirit helps us in our weakness. We do not know what we ought to pray for, but the Spirit himself intercedes for us through wordless groans.
>
> —ROMANS 8:26 (NIV)

One summer he encouraged me to plan a neighborhood carnival to raise money for muscular dystrophy. He helped me choose the games—simple, old-time favorites like pulling a string for a prize, popping a balloon with a dart, and dropping clothespins into a bottle—and to purchase the now-nostalgic penny-candy prizes, such as root beer barrels, Fruit Stripe gum, and mini juice-filled wax bottles. He wanted me to feel empowered and to believe that I had an important role to play in society and in serving others.

I remember feeling so proud of the event, and to this day I cannot help but feel this was the start of my lifelong love of volunteer service and event planning.

Through my teen years, Dad remained a steadfast protector, shielding me from the harshness of the world. His silent presence spoke volumes as he picked me up at the door to save my legs from the extra walking and made sure my physical needs were met at school.

> **Yet to all who did receive him, to those who believed in his name, he gave the right to become children of God.**
>
> —JOHN 1:12 (NIV)

I was told of a particular instance when he drove by my high school and happened to see me walking by myself within the fenced schoolyard. My classmates and I were required to walk a mile as part of a physical education class; because of my shorter legs and orthopedic issues, I struggled to complete the distance and, unsurprisingly, was the last student to finish.

This incident upset my dad so much that he, typically a man of few words, confronted the school administration. After that conversation, I was no longer required to fulfill the physical education requirements of my peers.

In my adulthood, Dad continued to be my anchor—driving me to college classes, aiding in landing my first job, and helping me find a place to live. He acted as a chauffeur and sat in the car reading the newspaper as he waited patiently for me to finish classes or jobs. No longer carrying me in his arms, he now did all he could to facilitate my success in discovering a world where my short stature did not define my capabilities.

Dad was not perfect, of course. None of us are. But his unconditional love, quiet demeanor, and humble spirit mirrored the godly values he instilled in me. Though I cannot recall him reciting specific Bible verses to me, I witnessed his faith being expressed in his actions and character.

★★★

In the nursing home that day, the joy of fond memories mingled with the stark reality of his current physical and mental state. As the Alzheimer's progressed, his health steadily declined to the point of needing help with simple daily tasks such as eating and dressing, and his memories faded to the point of no longer recognizing his loved ones, let alone knowing us by name.

> **Are not five sparrows sold for two pennies? Yet not one of them is forgotten by God.**
>
> **—LUKE 12:6 (NIV)**

Yet, amid the shadows of forgetfulness, I had a divine encounter with my dad that defied the limitations of the human mind. As I drew near to him, I looked up, being a foot and a half shorter than he was. I placed my hand into his, peered into his eyes, and smiled. In those solemn surroundings, Dad looked down, smiled back, and let out a cheerful "Hey, you!" For a fleeting moment, his eyes sparkled with recognition.

He recognized me. I had never expected to see him look at me that way again. In that moment we shared a supernatural connection that transcended the boundaries of comprehension, one I will forever cherish. Although he did not speak my name, I am certain he remembered me deep in his soul at that moment, and I knew without a doubt that it was a gift from God—a divine intercession that allowed him to momentarily break free from the chains of forgetfulness. When disease robbed my father and I of the ability to truly communicate, God gave us that moment of soul connection that ran deeper than words.

Though I didn't know it at the time, that was the last real interaction I would have with my father. A couple of weeks later, he was sent to the hospital, where he was unresponsive until he passed away shortly afterward. God knew. He gave me a memory to keep alongside all the other remembrances, a beautiful portrait forever etched in my mind.

Contributors

Acknowledgments

Every attempt has been made to credit the sources of copyrighted material used in this book. If any such acknowledgment has been inadvertently omitted or miscredited, receipt of such information would be appreciated.

Scripture quotations marked (ESV) are taken from *The Holy Bible, English Standard Version*. Copyright © 2001 by Crossway Bibles, a division of Good News Publishers. Used by permission. All rights reserved.

Scripture quotations marked (JPS) are taken from *Tanakh: A New Translation of the Holy Scriptures according to the Traditional Hebrew Text*. Copyright © 1985 by the Jewish Publication Society. All rights reserved.

Scripture quotations marked (KJV) are taken from the *King James Version of the Bible*.

Scripture quotations marked (MSG) are taken from *The Message*. Copyright © 1993, 2002, 2018 by Eugene H. Peterson.

Scripture quotations marked (NASB) are taken from the *New American Standard Bible*®, Copyright © 1960, 1971, 1977, 1995, 2020 by The Lockman Foundation. All rights reserved.

Scripture quotations marked (NIV) are taken from *The Holy Bible, New International Version*®, *NIV*®. Copyright © 1973, 1978, 1984, 2011 by Biblica, Inc. Used by permission. All rights reserved worldwide.

Scripture quotations marked (NKJV) are taken from the *New King James Version*®. Copyright © 1982 by Thomas Nelson. Used by permission. All rights reserved.

Scripture quotations marked (NLT) are taken from the *Holy Bible, New Living Translation*. Copyright © 1996, 2004, 2007, 2015 by Tyndale House Foundation. Used by permission of Tyndale House Publishers Inc., Carol Stream, Illinois. All rights reserved.

Scripture quotations marked (RSV) are taken from the *Revised Standard Version of the Bible*. Copyright © 1946, 1952, 1971 by the Division of Christian Education of the National Council of the Churches of Christ in the United States of America. Used by permission.

A Note from the Editors

We hope you enjoyed *Transformed by His Grace,* published by Guideposts. For more than seventy-five years, Guideposts, a nonprofit organization, has been driven by a vision of a world filled with hope. We aspire to be the voice of a trusted friend, a friend who makes you feel more hopeful and connected.

By making a purchase from Guideposts, you join our community in touching millions of lives, inspiring them to believe that all things are possible through faith, hope, and prayer. Your continued support allows us to provide uplifting resources to those in need. Whether through our communities, websites, apps, or publications, we inspire our audiences, bring them together, and comfort, uplift, entertain, and guide them. Visit us at guideposts.org to learn more.

We would love to hear from you. Write us at Guideposts, P.O. Box 5815, Harlan, Iowa 51593 or call us at (800) 932-2145. Did you love *Transformed by His Grace?* Leave a review for this product on guideposts.org/shop. Your feedback helps others in our community find relevant products.

Find inspiration, find faith, find Guideposts.

Shop our best sellers and favorites at
guideposts.org/shop

Or scan the QR code to go directly to our Shop